# The Complete Hyper Ketosis Diet

**Simple and Tasty Recipes Cookbook to Sustained Weight Loss, Optimal Health | 6-Week Meal Plan, and FAQ**

## Cecilia Snyder RD

**Disclaimer**

The information contained in this book is for educational and informational purposes only and is not intended as health or medical advice. The author and publisher are not responsible for any specific health or allergy needs that may require medical supervision and are not liable for any damages or negative consequences from any treatment, action, application, or preparation to any person reading or following the information in this book. References are provided for informational purposes only and do not constitute an endorsement of any websites or other sources.

# Table of Contents

# My Journey with the Hyper Ketosis Diet

Starting the Hyper Ketosis diet has been a life-changing journey for both my body and mind. When I first started, I had my doubts and hesitations. Like many, I was curious if this high-fat, low-carb approach would work for me, especially after trying countless diets that promised quick results but often led to disappointment. However, the more I learned about ketosis and its profound effects on the body, the more intrigued and motivated I became.

## The Beginning: Why I Chose Hyper Ketosis

Before starting the Hyper Ketosis diet, I struggled with energy fluctuations, cravings, and weight management. I would experience sugar highs followed by inevitable crashes, leaving me tired and irritable throughout the day. It was frustrating to feel so dependent on constant snacking to maintain energy. I realized it was time for a shift

After doing some research, I stumbled upon the ketogenic lifestyle. At first, the concept of eating more fats to lose fat seemed counterintuitive, but the science behind ketosis – using fat as the body's primary fuel source instead of carbohydrates – intrigued me. I decided to commit to the Hyper Ketosis diet to reset my metabolism, improve my energy levels, and finally achieve lasting weight loss.

## The Transition: Adapting to a New Way of Eating

The first few days on the diet were tough, but I learned a lot. Like many who start a ketogenic lifestyle, I experienced what is commonly referred to as the "keto flu." It's the body's natural response to the drastic reduction in carbs, leading to symptoms like fatigue, headaches, and irritability. Thankfully, I was prepared for this transition, and by increasing my electrolyte intake and staying hydrated, I managed to get through it.

As my body began to adapt to burning fat for fuel, I noticed significant changes. My energy levels started to stabilize. No more mid-afternoon crashes, no more constant hunger pangs. For the first time, I felt in control of my eating habits. The cravings for sugary snacks and carbs that had once been so overpowering were now gone.

## The Progress: Seeing Results

Within the first few weeks, the physical changes were undeniable. I lost several pounds of body fat, but what was more remarkable was how lean and toned I felt. I started to notice muscle definition, something I hadn't experienced in years. I noticed my clothes were fitting more comfortably, and I felt lighter on my feet.

But the benefits of the Hyper Ketosis diet went far beyond weight loss. I experienced mental clarity and focus like never before. Tasks that used to feel overwhelming became easier to manage, and I found myself being more productive and creative. My mood improved as well, as I no longer felt the irritability and mood swings that came with the highs and lows of a carb-heavy diet.

## Challenges Along the Way

Like any long-term journey, there were moments of doubt and temptation. Social events, family gatherings, and holidays posed challenges. It's not always easy to explain to others why you're avoiding certain foods, and there were times when I had to resist the temptation of desserts and bread.

However, I soon learned how to navigate these situations by planning ahead and bringing my own keto-friendly dishes to share. I realized that the benefits I was experiencing far outweighed any momentary indulgence. Whenever I felt like straying from the diet, I reminded myself of how far I had come and how much better I felt.

## Plateaus and Adjustments

One of the most challenging phases of my journey came when I hit a plateau. After losing a significant amount of weight and feeling great for months, my progress slowed, and I started to wonder if I had reached my limit. It was frustrating, but instead of giving up, I revisited my goals and made some adjustments.

I experimented with intermittent fasting, incorporating longer fasts to break through the plateau. I also tweaked my macronutrient ratios, slightly increasing my fat intake and adjusting my protein. These small changes made a big difference, and within a few weeks, I saw progress again, both in terms of weight loss and muscle definition.

## The Lifestyle: More Than Just a Diet

What started as a diet quickly became a lifestyle. The Hyper Ketosis approach isn't just about weight loss; it's about optimal health, energy, and longevity. Over time, I discovered that this way of eating is sustainable and adaptable. I learned how to prepare delicious keto-friendly meals that kept me satisfied and nourished, and I experimented with various recipes that fit my lifestyle.

I also incorporated exercise into my routine, focusing on strength training and low-intensity cardio, which complemented my ketogenic journey. The combination of ketosis and regular workouts helped me build lean muscle and maintain my fat loss.

## The End Result: A New Me

Today, I feel stronger, leaner, and more confident in my body. The weight I lost has stayed off, and I continue to enjoy the mental clarity, energy, and stability that the Hyper Ketosis diet provides. I no longer feel like I'm on a "diet" – it's simply the way I eat and live.

Reflecting on my journey, I realize that Hyper Ketosis has given me more than just physical results. It has reshaped my relationship with food, giving me control over my health and well-being. It has also taught me the importance of patience, perseverance, and adaptability. There were challenges along the way, but each one taught me something new about my body and my habits.

Advice for Others Considering Hyper Ketosis

If you're considering starting a Hyper Ketosis diet, my advice is to be patient with yourself and embrace the learning curve. The beginning may feel challenging, but once your body adapts, the benefits are incredible. Prepare yourself with knowledge, experiment with different foods and recipes, and don't be afraid to make adjustments along the way.

Most importantly, focus on the long-term. The Hyper Ketosis diet is not a quick fix; it's a powerful tool for lasting health and transformation. Stick with it, listen to your body, and enjoy the journey – because it's one that can truly change your life.

# Introduction

A cutting-edge approach to weight reduction and health improvement, the Hyper Ketosis Diet Plan is meant to take the advantages of regular ketogenic diets to the next level. It is designed to take dieting to a whole new level. It is possible for the Hyper Ketosis Diet to hasten the process of fat reduction, enhance mental clarity, increase energy levels, and promote general well-being. This is accomplished by concentrating on increasing the body's generation of ketones and accelerating the metabolism of fat.

In this introduction, we will explore the core concepts of Hyper Ketosis, breaking down how it works and why it is different from other low-carb or ketogenic diets. If you want to achieve your goals of losing weight, improving your mental concentration, or just leading a healthy lifestyle, the first step toward achieving success is to get an awareness of the principles of this metabolic state.

## Is hyper ketosis a condition?

An intensified condition of ketosis is referred to as hype ketosis. This is a state where the body is in ketosis, using fat for fuel instead of carbs, and producing ketones at a rapid pace. The goal of traditional ketogenic diets is to induce ketosis in the body by lowering the amount of carbohydrates consumed and instead increasing the amount of fat consumed. Hyper ketosis, on the other hand, goes beyond just that. In order to induce a more profound and long-lasting state of ketosis in the body, it is necessary to precisely adjust the proportions of macronutrients, which include carbs, proteins, and fats, in conjunction with certain lifestyle choices.

**In order to reach this "hyper" condition, one must:**

**Extremely low carbohydrate consumption:** Keeping daily carb intake below 20 grams or even fewer, to guarantee the body depends mostly on fat for energy.

**High-fat intake:** Increasing the amount of daily calories from fat to 75-85%, prompting the liver to make more ketones as an energy source.

**Moderate protein intake:** Controlling protein levels so as not to provoke gluconeogenesis (the process where excess protein is turned into glucose), which may disrupt ketosis.

In this heightened state of ketosis, the body becomes more effective at burning fat, not only from meals but also from stored fat stores. Hyper Ketosis is typically adopted by persons aiming for faster weight reduction, enhanced cognitive function, and other health advantages that come with prolonged, high-level ketone synthesis.

## How Hyper Ketosis Work

To understand how Hyper Ketosis works, it's vital to first comprehend the fundamentals of how the body makes and consumes energy.

### Energy Production and the Role of Carbohydrates

Under normal nutritional circumstances, the body predominantly utilizes glucose (sugar) as its major source of energy. This glucose originates from carbs found in meals like bread, pasta, fruit, and sweet snacks. When you ingest carbs, your body breaks them down into glucose, which is then utilized to energize cells, tissues, and organs.

However, when you dramatically cut your carbohydrate consumption, as in a ketogenic or Hyper Ketosis diet, your body must find another fuel source. Without enough glucose, the body goes into a metabolic condition known as ketosis.

### The Ketosis State: A Metabolic Shift

In ketosis, the liver starts to break down fat into molecules called ketones (particularly beta-hydroxybutyrate, acetoacetate, and acetone). These ketones become the predominant source of fuel for the body, particularly for the brain, which cannot directly consume fat for energy. Once the body adjusts to utilizing ketones effectively, this process may lead to various advantages, such as:

**Rapid fat loss:** Since the body is now burning fat for energy, both from dietary fats and stored fat, this might lead to a speedier decrease in body fat.

**Stable energy levels:** Unlike glucose, which may generate energy spikes and crashes, ketones give a stable and continuous energy source.

**Improved mental clarity:** Many individuals experience better attention and cognition owing to the brain's preference for ketones as a fuel source.

### Hyper Ketosis: Elevating the Ketosis Process

Hyper Ketosis is meant to optimize these advantages by driving the body into a greater ketone production state. This is done by fine-tuning the food and lifestyle to constantly favor fat metabolism over glucose. Here's how it works:

**Drastically Low Carbohydrate Intake:** Keeping carbs under 20 grams per day guarantees that glucose stays essentially inaccessible as an energy source. The body is therefore forced to depend nearly totally on fats for sustenance, which maintains it in a hyper-productive ketosis condition.

**Increased Fat Consumption:** Consuming 75-85% of your daily calories from fats allows the liver to consistently create ketones. This availability of fat guarantees there is always enough available to convert into ketones, sustaining a greater degree of ketosis.

**Moderating Protein Intake:** Protein is needed for muscle upkeep and bodily function, but too much may convert to glucose via gluconeogenesis. By retaining protein in reasonable amounts, Hyper Ketosis guarantees that the body doesn't switch to glucose metabolism, which would drive you out of ketosis.

**Supporting Lifestyle Factors:**

**Fasting:** Incorporating intermittent fasting or longer fasting intervals helps to further enhance ketone production. Fasting naturally depletes glucose storage and boosts fat burning, promoting ketosis.

**Exercise:** Physical exercise, particularly high-intensity or strength training, increases the depletion of glycogen (stored glucose), driving the body to burn fat for energy even quicker.

## Benefits of a Hyper Ketosis Diet

The Hyper Ketosis Diet is a highly specialized form of the ketogenic diet, intended to increase the body's capacity to burn fat and utilize ketones as a major energy source. While a regular ketogenic diet delivers numerous health advantages, the Hyper Ketosis method pushes these benefits even further by producing an amplified metabolic state. This section examines the primary advantages connected with the Hyper Ketosis Diet.

### 1. Accelerated Fat Loss

One of the most notable advantages of the Hyper Ketosis Diet is faster fat burning. When the body is in a state of ketosis, it goes from depending on carbs (glucose) for energy to utilizing fats. By enhancing ketone generation via very low carbohydrate intake and high-fat consumption, Hyper Ketosis supercharges this fat-burning process.

**Efficient Fat Utilization:** In Hyper Ketosis, your body becomes more proficient at using stored fat for energy. Since carbs are limited, the body taps into fat stores at a quicker rate than on a typical ketogenic diet, leading to faster and more significant fat loss.

**Reduced Hunger and Cravings:** The higher ketone levels may lower hunger and suppress cravings for sugary or carb-heavy meals, which can make it simpler to remain in a caloric deficit and remove extra weight.

### 2. Enhanced Mental Clarity and Focus

A fundamental component of the Hyper Ketosis Diet is its potential to boost brain function. The brain generally depends on glucose for energy, but when glucose is restricted, it adjusts to utilizing ketones as an alternate fuel source.

**Mental Clarity:** Many individuals experience greater mental concentration, improved memory, and increased cognitive function when in ketosis, particularly in the heightened condition of Hyper Ketosis. This is because ketones are a cleaner and more efficient fuel for the brain, giving a more consistent supply of energy than glucose.

**Reduced Brain Fog:** The absence of glucose spikes and crashes helps to normalize brain function, resulting in fewer energy dips and reduced brain fog throughout the day.

### 3. Increased Energy Levels

While certain diets may lead to energy swings owing to the dependence on carbohydrates and the inevitable crashes that accompany sugar intake, the Hyper Ketosis Diet gives continuous energy.

**Steady Energy Supply:** Since your body is continually breaking down fat into ketones for energy, it doesn't suffer the fast changes in energy that occur with a high-carb diet. This leads to more equal and maintained energy throughout the day, with fewer dips in energy levels.

**Improved Physical Endurance:** Athletes and active folks may discover that Hyper Ketosis boosts endurance. With a consistent supply of fat and ketones available for fuel, your body becomes more effective at powering through extended exercises or endurance sports without the need for carbohydrate loading.

### 4. Better Blood Sugar Regulation

Hyper Ketosis may have a substantial influence on blood sugar management, making it especially advantageous for persons with insulin resistance, type 2 diabetes, or metabolic syndrome.

**Stable Blood Glucose Levels:** By lowering carbohydrate consumption to practically nil, the Hyper Ketosis Diet avoids blood sugar rises and insulin surges. This helps to normalize blood sugar levels, which may be especially beneficial for controlling or even reversing insulin resistance.

**Improved Insulin Sensitivity:** Over time, the diet may improve insulin sensitivity, which is crucial for avoiding and controlling type 2 diabetes. With fewer carbohydrates to metabolize, the pancreas generates less insulin, and the body's cells become more sensitive to this hormone, allowing for better management of blood glucose.

### 5. Improved Metabolic Health

The Hyper Ketosis Diet may lead to beneficial changes in metabolic indicators, leading to overall improved health.

**Lower Inflammation:** Ketones have anti-inflammatory qualities, and adopting a Hyper Ketosis Diet may lower signs of inflammation in the body. Chronic inflammation is connected to a number of health concerns, including heart disease, obesity, and autoimmune diseases.

**Improved Lipid Profile:** Some persons notice improved cholesterol levels and triglyceride levels on a Hyper Ketosis Diet. The diet may improve levels of HDL (the "good" cholesterol) while reducing triglycerides, which is helpful for cardiovascular health.

### 6. Potential Therapeutic Benefits

There is increasing research showing that ketosis may have therapeutic effects beyond weight reduction and metabolic health.

**Neurological Benefits:** Ketosis is being examined as a possible therapy for neurological diseases such as epilepsy, Alzheimer's disease, and Parkinson's disease. The brain's preference for ketones over glucose may offer neuroprotective benefits.

**Cancer Prevention:** Some studies think that ketosis might have a role in reducing the development of some malignancies. Since cancer cells thrive on glucose, lowering glucose availability with a Hyper Ketosis Diet may prevent tumor development. However, additional study is required in this area.

## Who is This Diet For?

The Hyper Ketosis Diet is not for everyone, but it may be very useful for select people searching for certain health benefits. Below are the categories of persons who may benefit most from following this enhanced ketogenic strategy.

### 1. Individuals Seeking Rapid and Sustainable Weight Loss

People who have battled with reducing weight on regular diets may find the Hyper Ketosis Diet especially successful. This strategy promotes fat loss by improving the body's capacity to burn fat for fuel, making it a good option for:

**Those with a lot of weight to lose:** If you want to shed a considerable amount of body fat, the Hyper Ketosis Diet may help you accomplish your objectives quicker than a conventional low-calorie or even ordinary ketogenic diet.

**People with stubborn fat:** If you've reached a roadblock in your weight loss quest and can't seem to lose those last few pounds, boosting ketone production via Hyper Ketosis may give your metabolism the push it needs to break through that barrier.

### 2. People with Insulin Resistance or Type 2 Diabetes

The Hyper Ketosis Diet may be very effective for persons with blood sugar management difficulties.

**Improving Insulin Sensitivity:** People with insulin resistance or type 2 diabetes may benefit from the Hyper Ketosis Diet's ability to regulate blood sugar and enhance insulin sensitivity. With its very low carbohydrate consumption, the diet helps regulate blood glucose levels more successfully than most other dietary methods.

**Preventing Diabetes:** If you are prediabetic or have a family history of diabetes, adopting a Hyper Ketosis Diet may help avoid the advancement to full-blown diabetes by keeping your blood sugar and insulin levels under control.

### 3. Athletes and Fitness Enthusiasts

While many think that high-carb diets are needed for athletic performance, there is mounting evidence that the Hyper Ketosis Diet may actually promote high levels of physical activity and endurance.

**Endurance Athletes:** Those who participate in endurance sports, such as long-distance running or cycling, may benefit from the consistent energy source given by ketosis. The body's capacity to burn fat for fuel means athletes may go for longer durations without having to recharge with carbs.

**Bodybuilders and Strength Trainers:** Individuals focusing on growing muscle or retaining lean mass may also benefit from the Hyper Ketosis Diet. By ingesting proper quantities of protein and healthy fats, athletes may promote muscle maintenance while lowering body fat.

## 4. People Seeking Enhanced Mental Performance

For anybody wishing to increase mental clarity, attention, and cognitive performance, the Hyper Ketosis Diet may be suitable.

**Professionals and Students:** If you have work or studies that require lengthy periods of attention and concentration, Hyper Ketosis may aid by supplying a consistent stream of ketones to feed the brain, leading to heightened mental function.

**People with Neurodegenerative Conditions:** Those at risk of or coping with neurodegenerative disorders like Alzheimer's or Parkinson's may also find this diet advantageous since ketones have neuroprotective advantages that assist promote brain health.

## 5. Those Interested in Preventative Health

For those focusing on long-term health and illness prevention, the Hyper Ketosis Diet may provide tremendous advantages.

**Preventing Chronic Disease:** By reducing inflammation, improving metabolic health, and supporting better lipid profiles, this diet can play a role in preventing conditions like heart disease, stroke, and certain types of cancer.

**Aging Gracefully:** The diet's concentration on low-carb, anti-inflammatory foods may help manage age-related health issues, including cognitive loss and metabolic slowness.

## Key Components of the Hyper Ketosis Diet Plan

The Hyper Ketosis Diet is a specialized plan designed to maximize fat burning by putting the body into a deep state of ketosis. Achieving this heightened metabolic state involves a mix of careful macronutrient control, lifestyle behaviors, and supplements to ensure that the body stays in hyperkeratosis, burning fat effectively and creating a high quantity of ketones for energy.

In this part, we'll discuss the essential components of the Hyper Ketosis Diet, describing the nutritional, behavioral, and supplementary variables required for success.

### 1. Macronutrient Breakdown

The core of the Hyper Ketosis Diet is its unique macronutrient ratio, which stresses high fat, moderate protein, and extremely low carbs. Each of these macronutrients plays a key part in driving the body into a hyper state of ketosis when fat becomes the predominant fuel source.

### A. High-Fat Intake (75-85% of Daily Calories)

The key to developing and sustaining Hyper Ketosis is ingesting a significant quantity of fat. Fat serves as the major energy source in this diet, ensuring that the liver creates ketones to power the body and brain.

Fat as Fuel: In the absence of carbs, the body taps into dietary fat and stored fat stores to make ketones, which are subsequently utilized for energy. This is critical for sustaining hyperketosis since fat must continually be accessible for the liver to create ketones.

Healthy Fat Sources: The kind of fat you ingest is crucial. Focus on healthy fats that boost general well-being while optimizing ketone production:

Saturated Fats: Found in coconut oil, grass-fed butter, and animal fats, saturated fats may help raise ketone levels.

Monounsaturated Fats: These heart-healthy fats, found in olive oil, avocados, and almonds, give long-lasting energy and promote metabolic health.

Omega-3 Fatty Acids: Found in fatty fish like salmon, mackerel, and sardines, omega-3s help decrease inflammation and improve brain function.

## B. Moderate Protein Intake (15-20% of Daily Calories)

Protein is necessary for maintaining muscle growth, aiding tissue regeneration, and general body function, however, under the Hyper Ketosis Diet, protein consumption must be carefully monitored.

Avoiding Gluconeogenesis: Consuming too much protein might induce a process known as gluconeogenesis when the body turns extra protein into glucose. This may interrupt ketosis by giving the body with an alternate energy source (glucose), taking it out of the hyper-ketotic state. Therefore, protein consumption must be moderate—enough to maintain muscle, but not so much that it prevents ketosis.

High-Quality Protein Sources: Choose nutrient-dense, high-quality protein sources such as:

Grass-fed beef

Free-range chicken

Wild-caught fish

Organic eggs

Plant-based proteins including hemp, chia seeds, and low-carb almonds (for vegetarians)

## C. Very Low Carbohydrate Intake (5% or Less of Daily Calories)

The most crucial component of the Hyper Ketosis Diet is maintaining very low carbohydrate consumption. Carbohydrates must be reduced to guarantee that the body cannot depend on glucose for energy, pushing it to rely on fat and ketones instead.

Carb Restriction: Carbohydrate consumption is normally maintained below 20 grams per day in the Hyper Ketosis Diet, but some people may need to go even lower (below 10 grams) to sustain hyperketosis. The objective is to deplete glycogen reserves entirely, forcing the body into a profound state of fat burning.

Low-Carb, nutritional-dense Foods: To achieve nutritional demands while keeping carbohydrates low, emphasis on:

Leafy Greens: These leafy greens, spinach, kale, and arugula, are packed with vitamins and minerals and low in carbohydrates.

Cruciferous Vegetables: Broccoli, cauliflower, and Brussels sprouts are high in fiber and minerals while being low in carbs.

Berries: While most fruits are heavy in carbohydrates, modest portions of berries (such as raspberries and blackberries) are permitted in moderation owing to their low sugar content and strong antioxidant levels.

## 2. Incorporating Fasting and Meal Timing

Another key part of the Hyper Ketosis Diet is the planned use of fasting to promote ketone generation. Fasting stimulates the body to burn fat more quickly by depleting glucose stores and increasing dependence on ketones.

### A. Intermittent Fasting

Intermittent fasting (IF) is a key strategy in the Hyper Ketosis Diet. By confining eating to specified periods, you can:

Increase ketone production

Boost fat burning

Improve insulin sensitivity

Popular Fasting Methods:

16:8 Method: Fast for 16 hours and eat within an 8-hour interval. For example, eating from 12 PM to 8 PM and fasting from 8 PM to 12 PM the following day.

OMAD (One Meal a Day): This includes consuming all your daily calories in a single meal, and fasting for the remaining 23 hours.

### B. Extended Fasting

Extended fasts (lasting 24-72 hours) might further boost ketone levels and promote fat loss by extending the time the body spends in ketosis. While not essential for everyone, some people may benefit from lengthier fasting periods as part of their hyperketosis plan.

Autophagy: During lengthy fasts, the body enters a state called autophagy, when it starts to break down damaged cells and rebuild new ones. This procedure has been related to increased metabolic health, lifespan, and accelerated fat removal.


## 3. Ketogenic Foods and Meal Plans

Understanding which foods to eat is crucial to maintaining the Hyper Ketosis Diet. Below are major dietary categories and examples to help design a ketogenic meal plan.

### A. Healthy Fats

Coconut Oil: A high source of medium-chain triglycerides (MCTs), coconut oil is quickly turned into ketones.

Avocados: High in monounsaturated fats and fiber, they give continuous energy without boosting insulin.

Olive Oil: A nutritious fat that aids heart health and inflammation reduction.

### B. Proteins

Grass-Fed Meats: Rich in omega-3 fatty acids and CLA (conjugated linoleic acid), grass-fed meats build lean muscle and deliver critical nutrients.

Wild-Caught Fish: Salmon, mackerel, and sardines are good providers of omega-3 fatty acids, which boost brain function and prevent inflammation.

Eggs: A wonderful blend of fat and protein, eggs are versatile and nutrient-dense.

## C. Low-Carb Vegetables

Leafy Greens: Spinach, kale, and Swiss chard contain critical vitamins and minerals while being low in carbs.

Zucchini: A versatile vegetable that may be used as a pasta replacement or in casseroles.

Cauliflower: Low in carbohydrates and a wonderful alternative for rice or mashed potatoes in keto-friendly cooking.

## 4. Supplementation to Enhance Ketosis

To guarantee success on the Hyper Ketosis Diet, some supplements may assist your body's shift and help sustain high ketone levels.

## A. MCT Oil

MCT (medium-chain triglyceride) oil is a form of fat that is readily absorbed and turned into ketones by the liver, making it a beneficial supplement for individuals on a Hyper Ketosis Diet. MCT oil can:

Increase ketone production

Provide fast energy

Suppress hunger

## B. Exogenous Ketones

Exogenous ketone supplements (such as beta-hydroxybutyrate or BHB salts) give an immediate supply of ketones, helping to boost blood ketone levels and enhance mental clarity, particularly during the first stages of ketosis.

## C. Electrolytes

When following a low-carb diet, the body loses electrolytes more rapidly due to lower insulin levels and water loss. It's vital to complement with:

Sodium: Found in bone broth or Himalayan salt, sodium helps retain hydration.

Potassium: Found in leafy greens and avocados, potassium enhances muscular function and reduces cramping.

Magnesium: Magnesium supplements or magnesium-rich foods like pumpkin seeds may help avoid exhaustion, muscular cramps, and headaches.

## D. Digestive Enzymes

High-fat diets may often be problematic for digestion, particularly for individuals migrating from a higher-carb diet. Digestive enzymes that break down lipids, proteins, and carbohydrates may aid enhance digestion and nutrition absorption.

## 5. Exercise to Support Hyper Ketosis

While nutrition plays a crucial part in establishing Hyper Ketosis, exercise may further boost the process by emptying glycogen reserves, encouraging fat loss, and enhancing insulin sensitivity.

## A. High-Intensity Interval Training (HIIT)

HIIT incorporates short bursts of intensive activity followed by shorter recovery intervals. This sort of training may rapidly deplete glycogen reserves, prompting the body to turn to fat for energy. It's particularly effective in combination with a ketogenic diet for fat-burning and retaining muscular mass.

## B. Strength Training

Lifting weights helps preserve lean muscular mass and increases metabolism. It also helps enhance insulin sensitivity, which is vital for remaining in ketosis and regulating blood sugar levels.

## C. Low-Intensity Cardio

Activities like walking, cycling, and swimming may enhance fat burning without emptying glycogen reserves. These workouts are particularly good for people trying to remain in ketosis while keeping a balanced fitness plan.

## 6. Monitoring Ketosis

Achieving and sustaining hyper ketosis involves meticulous monitoring to ensure that your body is continually generating a high quantity of ketones.

## A. Ketone Testing Methods

Blood Ketone Meters: The most accurate approach to test ketone levels is with a blood ketone meter. It detects the quantity of beta-hydroxybutyrate (BHB), the major ketone in the circulation.

Breath Ketone Meters: Breath ketone meters detect acetone levels in the breath, which might indicate the presence of ketones.

Urine Strips: While less precise, urine strips test acetoacetate, a form of ketone excreted in the urine.

## B. Target Ketone Levels

In hyper ketosis, the objective is to maintain ketone levels between 1.5 and 3.0 mmol/L. This range guarantees that the body is effectively burning fat for fuel, improving energy levels, mental clarity, and fat reduction.

The Hyper Ketosis Diet Plan is a complete, science-based method to achieve deep and prolonged ketosis for maximal fat-burning and metabolic advantages.

# Chapter 1: The Science of Ketosis

The Hyper Ketosis Diet is predicated around a profound knowledge of ketosis—a natural metabolic condition that occurs when the body burns fat for fuel instead of carbs. To completely comprehend the advantages and mechanics of the Hyper Ketosis Diet, it's vital to understand the science underlying ketosis, how it differs from hazardous states like ketoacidosis, and how the body reaches this fat-burning state.

## Understanding Ketosis: The Basics

Ketosis is a metabolic condition that happens when your body does not have enough carbs to burn for energy, so it begins breaking down stored fat into molecules called ketones to utilize as fuel. In this condition, the body becomes extraordinarily effective at burning fat, which is the cornerstone of the ketogenic diet and the Hyper Ketosis Diet Plan.

### A. How the Body Enters Ketosis

Under normal nutritional circumstances, the body's principal source of energy comes from glucose, a kind of sugar obtained from carbs. When you consume meals heavy in carbohydrates, your body turns these carbs into glucose, which enters the circulation and is subsequently transferred to your cells for energy. The hormone insulin plays a critical function here since it helps control blood sugar levels and ensures glucose is taken into cells.

When carbohydrate consumption is severely decreased (as in the case of a ketogenic diet), the body's glucose stores begin to dwindle. After 24 to 48 hours of carb restriction, glycogen (the stored form of glucose) is practically spent. The liver subsequently proceeds to break down fatty acids into ketone bodies—acetoacetate, beta-hydroxybutyrate (BHB), and acetone—to be utilized as an alternative energy source. This process is known as ketogenesis, and it is the main force underlying ketosis.

In a condition of ketosis, ketones replace glucose as the body's principal fuel source. This alteration in energy metabolism is what allows for enhanced fat-burning and weight reduction, as well as several other health advantages linked with ketosis.

### B. The Role of the Liver in Ketosis

The liver plays a crucial function in ketosis. It's the organ responsible for creating ketones from stored fat via a process called beta-oxidation. During beta-oxidation, fatty acids are broken down into acetyl-CoA, which is subsequently transformed into ketones. These ketones may then move through the circulation to supply energy to the brain, muscles, and other tissues.

Why the Brain Prefers Ketones in Ketosis: The brain is one of the most energy-demanding organs, often needing roughly 120 grams of glucose per day. However, during ketosis, the brain may obtain most of its energy from ketones, notably BHB. This transition to ketones is one of the essential aspects of ketosis since it permits the body to continue operating effectively even with decreased carbohydrate intake.

## C. How Long Does It Take to Enter Ketosis?

For most people, it takes around 2 to 4 days of rigorous carbohydrate restriction (under 50 grams of carbohydrates per day) to enter ketosis. However, this time period might vary based on things like:

Carbohydrate intake: The less carbohydrates you consume, the sooner you'll enter ketosis.

Activity level: Regular exercise, particularly high-intensity activities, may deplete glycogen reserves quicker and hasten the shift to ketosis.

Metabolic health: Individuals with insulin resistance or metabolic problems may take longer to achieve ketosis, since their systems may be less effective at switching from glucose to fat for energy.

Once in ketosis, the body continues to make ketones as long as carbohydrate consumption is low and fat intake is adequate to fuel the process.

## The Difference Between Ketosis and Ketoacidosis

While ketosis is a typical and healthy metabolic state, there is sometimes a misunderstanding between ketosis and a severe illness termed ketoacidosis. Although they seem similar, ketosis and ketoacidosis are two very distinct metabolic states, with ketoacidosis being a life-threatening illness commonly encountered in uncontrolled diabetes or alcohol addiction. Understanding the difference between the two is crucial to ensure that ketosis is performed safely and efficiently.

## A. What is Ketoacidosis?

Ketoacidosis—more specifically diabetic ketoacidosis (DKA)—is a severe and potentially fatal condition that occurs when the body produces dangerously high levels of ketones, leading to acidic blood pH. This state is most commonly seen in people with type 1 diabetes, but it can also occur in type 2 diabetes under certain conditions, as well as in cases of alcohol-induced ketoacidosis.

In DKA, the body's insulin production is either very low or nonexistent, which prevents glucose from entering the cells for energy. As a consequence, the body starts breaking down fat at a quick speed, resulting in a large overproduction of ketones. In contrast to nutritional ketosis, when ketone levels are mild (usually between 0.5 and 3.0 mmol/L), in ketoacidosis, ketone levels may increase to 10 mmol/L or more. This excess of ketones leads the blood to become excessively acidic, leading to hazardous imbalances in electrolytes, dehydration, and damage to key organs.

**Symptoms of Diabetic Ketoacidosis:**

Nausea and vomiting

Severe abdominal pain

Excessive thirst and frequent urination

Confusion or trouble thinking clearly

Rapid breathing and fruity-smelling breath (due to acetone)

Fatigue and weakness

Coma (in extreme situations)

Ketoacidosis is a medical emergency that needs prompt treatment, often requiring insulin therapy, fluid replenishment, and electrolyte balance.

### B. Why Nutritional Ketosis is Safe

Unlike other metabolic states, nutritional ketosis, achieved through a ketogenic diet, is a controlled and beneficial condition. During nutritional ketosis, the body creates ketones at moderate levels, which are utilized effectively for energy without causing damage to the body's acid-base balance. In this condition, the blood stays slightly alkaline or neutral, and there are no harmful surges in ketone levels.

## Key Differences Between Ketosis and Ketoacidosis:

### Insulin Levels:

In ketoacidosis, insulin levels are either absent or significantly low, leading to uncontrolled fat breakdown and ketone generation.

In ketosis, insulin levels are low yet present, helping regulate fat breakdown and ketone generation in a regulated way.

### Ketone Levels:

In ketoacidosis, ketone levels increase to harmful levels (over 10 mmol/L), leading the blood to turn acidic.

In ketosis, ketone levels are normally between 0.5 to 3.0 mmol/L, which is within a safe and regulated range for fat burning and energy generation.

### Blood pH:

In ketoacidosis, the blood becomes acidic owing to the excessive amount of ketones, resulting in a pH level below 7.35.

In ketosis, the blood pH stays steady (about 7.35 to 7.45), since ketone generation is balanced and controlled.

### Who is at Risk:

Ketoacidosis often affects persons with type 1 diabetes, type 2 diabetes, or serious alcohol addiction issues.

Ketosis may be safely attained by healthy adults using a well-formulated ketogenic diet, even in those with type 2 diabetes under medical supervision.

### C. Nutritional Ketosis: The Body's Built-In Safety Mechanism

The body has various built-in mechanisms that prevent nutritional ketosis from escalating into hazardous ketoacidosis. For example, the presence of insulin and glucagon—two hormones that govern blood sugar and fat metabolism—ensures that fat breakdown and ketone synthesis stay under control. Additionally, the kidneys eliminate extra ketones in the urine, helping to maintain regulated ketone levels in the circulation.

For most individuals without underlying metabolic issues, dietary ketosis is not only safe but also very advantageous. It enhances fat burning, mental clarity, and general metabolic health without offering the hazards associated with ketoacidosis.

## Ketones: Your Body's Alternative Fuel Source

One of the most fundamental characteristics of a ketogenic diet—and notably the Hyper Ketosis Diet—is that it converts the body's major fuel source from carbs to ketones, which are created from fat. Understanding how ketones operate and the role they play in the body is key to maximizing the advantages of ketosis.

### A. What Are Ketones?

Ketones, also termed ketone bodies, are water-soluble molecules created in the liver during the process of fat metabolism. They are formed when the body breaks down fatty acids to utilize as fuel in the absence of adequate glucose from carbs. This occurs during times of fasting, heavy activity, or while following a low-carbohydrate diet such as the ketogenic or Hyper Ketosis Diet.

**There are three basic kinds of ketones:**

**Acetoacetate (AcAc):** The first ketone body formed during ketosis. It may either be utilized directly as energy or transformed into beta-hydroxybutyrate.

**Beta-hydroxybutyrate (BHB):** Although technically not a genuine ketone owing to its chemical structure, BHB is regarded as the most efficient and steady energy source for the brain and muscles.

**Acetone:** A consequence of acetoacetate breakdown, acetone is less helpful as an energy source and is frequently expelled via urine or breath, which creates the distinctive "fruity" fragrance of someone in ketosis.

When carbohydrate consumption is limited, as in the Hyper Ketosis Diet, the liver boosts its synthesis of ketones to offer an alternate energy source for the body, notably the brain, which generally depends on glucose. Ketones function as an efficient and potent fuel, delivering sustained energy levels and encouraging fat reduction, mental clarity, and metabolic advantages.

### B. How Ketones Fuel the Body

When the body is in ketosis, it changes from utilizing glucose to ketones and fatty acids as its major energy source. Here's how ketones act in various regions of the body:

**The Brain:** While the brain normally depends on glucose, it may utilize ketones, especially BHB, as an alternate fuel. This is important because the brain can't use fat directly as fuel. Once the body is accustomed to utilizing ketones, the brain may obtain up to 75% of its energy from ketones, resulting in better cognitive performance, mental clarity, and attention.

**The Muscles:** Muscles can utilize both fatty acids and ketones for fuel, making them more effective during strenuous activity. BHB, in particular, is a fantastic source of energy for muscle tissue, enhancing endurance and performance during exercises.

**The Heart and Other Organs:** The heart and kidneys prefer ketones as a fuel source because they deliver more energy per unit of oxygen than glucose. This greater efficiency may contribute to better cardiac function and overall metabolic health.

**C. Benefits of Ketones as a Fuel Source**

**Enhanced Fat Burning:** Since ketones are created by breaking down fat storage, ketosis promotes greater fat burning, making it an optimal condition for weight reduction and body recompositing.

**Sustained Energy:** Unlike glucose, which produces variations in blood sugar levels, ketones offer a steady and sustained source of energy. This helps prevent energy crashes and enhances overall stamina.

**Mental Clarity and Focus:** Ketones, particularly BHB, are very efficient in fueling the brain. Many persons on a ketogenic diet report better attention, concentration, and cognitive performance as a consequence.

**Reduced Inflammation:** Ketones have been demonstrated to decrease signs of inflammation in the body, which may help lessen the risk of chronic illnesses and enhance recovery after workouts.

**Appetite Suppression:** Ketones, especially BHB, are known to lower appetite by altering hunger hormones such as ghrelin and leptin. This may make it simpler to sustain a calorie deficit and accomplish weight reduction objectives.

**Increased Physical Performance:** By utilizing fat and ketones for fuel, the body becomes more effective at burning fat during exercise, enhancing endurance, and minimizing the need for carbohydrate loading before workouts.

## How to Measure and Track Ketosis

Achieving and sustaining ketosis is a continuous process that needs constant monitoring. Monitoring your ketone levels guarantees that your body stays in the appropriate range for ketosis and helps you adapt your food and lifestyle to optimize the advantages. There are numerous techniques to quantify ketones in the body, each having its merits and downsides.

**A. Blood Ketone Testing**

Blood ketone meters are the most reliable way to measure ketone levels, particularly beta-hydroxybutyrate (BHB) levels, in the blood. This procedure is similar to how diabetics assess blood sugar levels and entails using a tiny lancet to prick the finger, take a drop of blood, and analyze it with a ketone test strip.

**Pros:**

Highly precise and dependable, delivering a direct measure of BHB, the most significant ketone body.

Provides real-time readings, making it simple to measure ketone levels throughout the day.

**Cons:**

Requires acquiring a ketone meter and test strips, which might be pricey.

Involves pricking the finger, which may not be acceptable for everyone.

**Optimal Ketone Range for Hyper Ketosis:**

In nutritional ketosis, ketone levels typically range from 0.5 to 3.0 mmol/L. However, for individuals following the Hyper Ketosis Diet, the goal range is between 1.5 and 3.0 mmol/L, since this is where the body best burns fat for energy and obtains the metabolic advantages of ketosis.

**B. Breath Ketone Testing**

Breath ketone meters detect the quantity of acetone in the breath, which is a consequence of fat breakdown in ketosis. This procedure is less intrusive than blood testing and does not need test strips. The user just breathes into the meter, which examines the amount of acetone present.

**Pros:**

Non-invasive, no need for finger pricking or test strips.

Once you acquire the gadget, there are no extra fees.

**Cons:**

Less accurate than blood ketone testing, since it only detects acetone, not BHB.

May offer variable readings dependent on hydration, alcohol consumption, or other circumstances.

**Optimal Ketone Range:**

Breath ketone meters frequently report measurements in parts per million (ppm). In general, a value of 10-40 ppm suggests moderate to high degrees of ketosis, however, the specific ranges may vary by instrument.

**C. Urine Ketone Testing**

Urine ketone strips are the most economical and accessible tool for testing ketosis. These strips measure acetoacetate, a type of ketone found in urine. Users just dip the strip into a urine sample, and the color shift on the strip reveals the number of ketones present.

**Pros:**

Inexpensive and commonly accessible in pharmacies.

Easy to use and needs no additional equipment.

**Cons:**

Less accurate than blood or breath tests, particularly when the body adjusts to ketosis. As you grow more effective at utilizing ketones, fewer ketones are discharged in the urine, leading to lower values even if you are in ketosis.

Results might be altered by hydration levels.

**Optimal Ketone Range:**

The color on the strip will vary from pale pink to deep purple, with deeper hues indicating greater amounts of ketones. However, urine testing is best performed during the first phases of ketosis and may become less trustworthy as you become keto-adapted.

**D. How Often to Test Ketone Levels**

For people on the Hyper Ketosis Diet, it's crucial to frequently measure ketone levels to ensure you are in the optimum range. Here's a proposed testing schedule:

Daily Testing: If you're new to the diet, testing once a day, especially in the morning, will help you monitor your progress and ensure you're remaining in ketosis.

**Post-Meal Testing:** You may wish to test 1 to 2 hours after meals, particularly if you're experimenting with new foods or modifying macronutrient ratios, to see how they affect your ketone levels.

**After Exercise:** Testing ketone levels after exercise may give information about how physical activity affects your ketosis. For some, hard activity may temporarily drop ketone levels, while others may observe an increase owing to accelerated fat metabolism.

## Common Myths About Ketosis

The ketogenic diet, and particularly its more sophisticated variation, the Hyper Ketosis Diet, has increased in popularity in recent years. However, despite its effectiveness in helping many people achieve weight reduction, better mental clarity, and other health advantages, there are various misunderstandings and fallacies regarding ketosis. These fallacies sometimes come from misunderstandings about how the body operates in a low-carbohydrate condition or from generalizations based on obsolete nutritional ideas. Let's investigate and refute some of the most frequent fallacies regarding ketosis.

**Myth 1: Ketosis Is Dangerous and Leads to Ketoacidosis**

One of the most frequent fallacies about ketosis is that it is hazardous and might lead to a life-threatening illness called ketoacidosis. This misperception generally originates from a misinterpretation between nutritional ketosis and diabetic ketoacidosis (DKA), two completely distinct metabolic states.

**Nutritional Ketosis:** When following a ketogenic diet, the body enters a regulated state of ketosis in which it burns fat for fuel and creates ketones. Ketone levels normally stay in the range of 0.5 to 3.0 mmol/L in nutritional ketosis, which is considered safe and healthy. This process helps the body adapt to utilize fat as a major fuel source, delivering advantages including weight reduction, consistent energy levels, and cognitive improvement.

**Diabetic Ketoacidosis (DKA):** DKA is a hazardous illness that develops in persons with untreated type 1 diabetes or, rarely, type 2 diabetes. In DKA, the body creates abnormally high quantities of ketones (typically above 10 mmol/L) owing to a severe shortage of insulin, leading the blood to turn acidic. This situation necessitates urgent medical intervention.

**The Truth:** Nutritional ketosis is a normal and harmless metabolic state that does not induce ketoacidosis in healthy persons. The two situations are fundamentally different, and ketosis should not be considered a harmful state when treated appropriately. For most individuals without diabetes, the body has built-in systems to control ketone synthesis, ensuring that levels remain within a healthy range.

## Myth 2: You Need to Eat High Protein to Stay in Ketosis

Another prevalent myth is that in order to sustain ketosis, you need to eat a high-protein diet. Some individuals feel that protein is important to fuel muscle development and prevent muscle loss, which drives them to overconsume protein when following a ketogenic diet. However, this technique might be harmful to reaching and sustaining ketosis.

**Protein and Gluconeogenesis:** While protein is vital for mending tissues and creating muscle, too much protein might actually interfere with ketosis. When protein consumption is high, the body turns extra protein into glucose via a process called gluconeogenesis. This may elevate blood sugar levels and limit the generation of ketones, possibly knocking the body out of ketosis.

**The Right Balance:** On a ketogenic or Hyper Ketosis Diet, it's crucial to maintain a modest protein consumption. The diet generally consists of 70-80% fat, 20-25% protein, and 5-10% carbs. This balance ensures that the body gets enough fat to make ketones while still delivering appropriate protein to maintain muscle mass and promote general health.

**The Truth:** High protein consumption is not essential to remain in ketosis. In fact, extra protein might impede your capacity to make ketones and sustain ketosis. Focus on ingesting a minimal quantity of protein, and let fat act as your major energy source.

## Myth 3: You Can't Build Muscle While in Ketosis

A widespread misunderstanding is that it's hard to gain muscle when following a ketogenic diet since the body purportedly needs carbs for muscular growth. Many individuals assume that you need huge quantities of carbs to sustain intensive exercises and assist muscle synthesis. However, this is not totally accurate.

**Ketosis and Muscle Preservation:** In ketosis, the body becomes very efficient at consuming fat and ketones for fuel. Contrary to common assumption, the body does not need carbs for muscle development. Protein synthesis, the process by which muscles heal and expand, may proceed in a low-carbohydrate environment as long as appropriate protein is ingested.

**Hormonal Balance:** A ketogenic diet helps maintain appropriate levels of hormones including insulin and growth hormone, both of which play a critical role in muscle building and fat metabolism. While insulin is essential for muscle development, ketosis enables the body to attain a balance of anabolic hormones without excess carbohydrate consumption.

**Strength exercise:** Studies have shown that persons on a ketogenic diet may grow and retain muscle mass while shedding fat, particularly when participating in regular resistance exercise. Some professional athletes and bodybuilders adopt ketogenic diets and obtain outstanding muscle development and performance outcomes.

**The Truth:** You can grow muscle while following a ketogenic diet, provided you eat enough protein and participate in resistance exercise. Ketones and fat may fuel exercises and boost muscle building just as well as carbs.

## Myth 4: Ketosis Causes Nutrient Deficiencies

Some detractors of the ketogenic diet believe that it is extremely restricted and may lead to dietary shortages, notably in vitamins and minerals found in fruits, vegetables, and grains. While it's true that a badly designed ketogenic diet might result in inadequate micronutrient consumption, a well-balanced ketogenic diet gives enough nourishment.

**Vegetable Intake:** Despite the carbohydrate limitation, a ketogenic diet promotes the eating of non-starchy vegetables such as spinach, broccoli, cauliflower, zucchini, and kale. These veggies are low in carbohydrates yet high in vital vitamins, minerals, and fiber, helping avoid nutritional deficits.

**Healthy Fats:** A ketogenic diet encourages the intake of healthy fats, such as avocados, nuts, seeds, olive oil, and fatty seafood like salmon. These meals are nutrient-dense and include critical fatty acids, vitamins, and minerals that are crucial for heart health, cognitive function, and general well-being.

**Supplements:** In circumstances when specific nutrients are difficult to get from food sources alone, supplements like magnesium, potassium, and omega-3 fatty acids may assist cover any gaps in the diet.

**The Truth:** A well-planned ketogenic diet that includes a range of nutrient-dense foods may deliver all the critical vitamins and minerals required for optimum health. It's crucial to concentrate on eating complete, unprocessed foods and including a broad mix of veggies, healthy fats, and proteins.

## Myth 5: The Ketogenic Diet Is Only for Weight Loss

While it's true that the ketogenic diet is particularly successful for weight reduction, this is simply one of its many advantages. Ketosis provides a variety of health gains beyond dropping pounds, making it suited for persons pursuing diverse health goals.

**Metabolic Health:** The ketogenic diet may help increase insulin sensitivity and manage blood sugar levels, making it a useful strategy for treating type 2 diabetes and avoiding metabolic illnesses.

**Cognitive Function:** Ketones offer a consistent and efficient supply of energy for the brain, which helps increase mental clarity, attention, and memory. Research shows that the ketogenic diet may also have significant advantages for neurological diseases including Alzheimer's disease and epilepsy.

**Inflammation and Heart Health:** The ketogenic diet has been demonstrated to decrease signs of inflammation in the body, which may help lessen the risk of chronic illnesses such as heart disease and some malignancies. It also helps heart health by decreasing cholesterol levels and reducing triglycerides.

**The Truth:** The ketogenic diet is much more than simply a weight-loss technique. It has several health advantages, including enhanced metabolic health, cognitive function, and lower inflammation. It's a dynamic approach to health that may be customized to numerous aims beyond weight control.

**Myth 6: Carbs Are Essential for Energy**

One of the most persistent beliefs is that carbohydrates are important for energy, particularly for athletes and those engaged in high-intensity activity. Many people assume that without carbs, the body would lack the fuel it needs to work efficiently. However, ketosis indicates that the body can function without a substantial intake of carbohydrates.

**Fat as Fuel:** Once the body is accustomed to ketosis, it becomes very efficient at utilizing fat and ketones as its principal sources of energy. This delivers a constant, long-lasting energy source, without the peaks and crashes associated with carbohydrate ingestion.

**Endurance Athletes:** Many endurance athletes adopt a ketogenic diet to increase their performance by depending on fat for fuel. Fat delivers more energy per gram than carbs, enabling athletes to maintain physical exercise for longer durations without the need for continual glucose replacement.

**The Truth:** Carbohydrates are not required for energy. Once accustomed to ketosis, the body effectively utilizes fat and ketones as its principal energy sources, providing prolonged, consistent energy for both everyday activities and athletic performance.

Starting a Hyper Ketosis Diet involves careful preparation and a clear grasp of how to move your body into ketosis. This advanced variation of the ketogenic diet is meant to enhance fat-burning capacity, improve cognitive function, and boost general health by sustaining a deeper state of ketosis. However, the adjustment may be tough for people new to low-carbohydrate diets, so it's crucial to prepare your body and mind for the trip ahead.

This chapter will lead you through the beginning phases of adopting a Hyper Ketosis Diet, including prepping your body for ketosis, establishing realistic objectives, and managing expectations for the process.

## Preparing Your Body for Ketosis

The move from a high-carbohydrate diet to one that is highly dependent on fats for energy may be a shock to your system, especially in the first few days. Understanding the changes your body will go through and taking action to prepare will assist ease this transition.

### 1. Gradual Carbohydrate Reduction

One of the first stages in preparing your body for ketosis is progressively limiting your carbohydrate consumption. Instead of eliminating carbohydrates significantly overnight, which may cause considerable

pain for some, adopt a step-by-step strategy to ease your body into fat adaption.

**Week 1:** Start by removing apparent sources of refined carbs including bread, spaghetti, and sugary snacks. Instead, concentrate on entire meals that are naturally lower in carbs such as leafy greens, non-starchy veggies, and healthy fats.

**Week 2:** Reduce your daily carb consumption further, aiming for roughly 50-75 grams per day. This will help your body to acclimate to decreased blood sugar levels and begin the process of moving into ketosis.

**Week 3:** Once you've accustomed to eating less carbs, drop your consumption to the average ketogenic range of 20-50 grams of net carbohydrates per day. This will help you enter ketosis and start creating ketones for energy.

### 2. Increase Healthy Fats

To properly enter and sustain ketosis, your body has to depend on dietary fats as its major source of energy. In the Hyper Ketosis Diet, this stage is vital, since fats will fuel most of your activities and metabolic processes.

Focus on eating healthy fats such as avocados, olive oil, coconut oil, nuts, seeds, butter, and fatty seafood like salmon. These fats are nutrient-dense and will help you feel full while lowering the danger of consuming carbs.

Incorporating sources of medium-chain triglycerides (MCTs), such as coconut oil or MCT oil, might be advantageous. MCTs are swiftly turned into ketones by the liver, providing an instant energy source and helping to speed up the process of ketosis.

### 3. Optimize Electrolytes and Hydration

One of the most frequent issues individuals have while beginning a ketogenic diet is the "keto flu," a collection of symptoms that might include exhaustion, headaches, muscular cramps, and irritability. This happens because of the body's quick depletion of glycogen and water storage, which also causes a loss of critical electrolytes such as sodium, potassium, and magnesium.

To lessen the pain of keto flu and maintain your body working properly:

**Increase your salt intake:** As you lose water weight, your body will also lose sodium. Adding additional salt to your meals, drinking bone broth, or utilizing electrolyte supplements will help recover this lost sodium.

**Magnesium and potassium:** Incorporate magnesium-rich foods like leafy greens, nuts, and seeds into your diet. Potassium-rich foods such as avocados, spinach, and salmon will also assist in maintaining adequate electrolyte balance.

**Stay hydrated:** Make sure to drink enough of water throughout the day, since dehydration may increase symptoms of the keto flu. Aim for at least 8-10 glasses of water every day and consider increasing your consumption during times of activity or hot weather.

### 4. Adapt Your Exercise Routine

In the first few weeks of converting to a Hyper Ketosis Diet, your body may not perform efficiently during high-intensity exercises owing to the limited availability of glycogen. It's normal to notice a short drop in endurance or strength as your body adjusts to using fat and ketones for energy.

**Low-Intensity Workouts:** During the adaption period, concentrate on low-intensity exercises like walking, yoga, or mild strength training. These activities will help your body burn fat without exhausting glycogen reserves.

**High-Intensity Exercise:** As your body becomes fat-adapted and more effective at utilizing ketones for fuel, you may gradually resume higher-intensity activities like as weightlifting, sprinting, or interval training.

## Setting Goals and Expectations

When beginning any new diet or lifestyle change, creating clear and realistic objectives is vital for long-term success. The Hyper Ketosis Diet is no exception. Defining your objectives and knowing what to anticipate along your trip can help you remain motivated, measure progress, and alter your strategy as required.

### 1. Define Your Objectives

Before delving into the Hyper Ketosis Diet, take some time to properly identify your objectives. These might encompass a variety of aims, such as:

**Weight Loss:** Many persons start a ketogenic diet with the main purpose of decreasing body fat. Ketosis naturally stimulates fat burning, but it's crucial to establish a realistic timescale for weight reduction. Aim for gradual improvement rather than anticipating spectacular outcomes within a few weeks.

**Enhanced Cognitive Function:** Ketones offer a consistent, efficient energy supply for the brain, and many individuals report enhanced mental clarity, attention, and productivity when in ketosis. If this is one of your objectives, assess how you feel psychologically while your body adjusts to the diet.

**Better Blood Sugar Control:** If you're treating prediabetes, type 2 diabetes, or insulin resistance, ketosis may help stabilize blood sugar levels. Set objectives linked to lowering blood sugar swings or increasing insulin sensitivity over time.

**Increased Energy:** Once your body adjusts to utilizing fat for fuel, you should enjoy more constant energy levels throughout the day, without the highs and lows associated with a high-carbohydrate diet.

**Physical Performance:** If you're an athlete or fitness enthusiast, you may desire to boost your endurance and performance. While there may be an initial fall in performance during the acclimation period, many athletes find that ketosis promotes sustained energy throughout long-duration activity.

## 2. Set Short-Term and Long-Term Goals

To sustain motivation and measure success, it's necessary to establish both short-term and long-term objectives for your Hyper Ketosis journey.

**Short-Term Goals:** These might include milestones like entering ketosis, controlling symptoms of the keto flu, or losing the first few pounds. Setting modest, manageable objectives can help you experience a feeling of achievement early on.

**Long-Term Goals:** Over the course of many months, you may establish bigger targets like attaining your target weight, increasing your metabolic health, or boosting sports performance. Remember that the Hyper Ketosis Diet is a long-term lifestyle, thus improvement may be modest but sustained.

## 3. Manage Your Expectations

While the Hyper Ketosis Diet offers various advantages, it's crucial to recognize that outcomes might vary depending on individual aspects such as metabolism, exercise level, age, and health issues. Managing your expectations and being patient with the process will avoid disappointment or frustration.

**Weight reduction:** While ketosis is helpful for fat reduction, the first weight you lose is generally attributable to water loss when your body depletes glycogen reserves. After this first decline, fat loss will proceed at a slower but consistent rate. It's typical for weight reduction to fluctuate from week to week, so concentrate on long-term trends rather than daily variations on the scale.

**Keto Flu:** Many individuals suffer modest symptoms in the first week, such as lethargy, headaches, or irritability. These symptoms are transitory and normally fade after your body learns to utilize ketones for fuel.

**Plateaus:** It's typical to endure weight reduction plateaus or times of slower progress. This is part of the process, and making tiny tweaks to your diet or workout program might help you break through these plateaus.

**Energy Levels:** Some individuals feel lethargic or sluggish during the first few days or weeks of shifting into ketosis. However, as your body grows more effective at burning fat for fuel, you will likely experience increased and consistent energy levels.

### 4. Track Your Progress

Monitoring your progress is a powerful way to stay motivated and see how your body responds to the Hyper Ketosis Diet.

**Measuring Ketones:** Use instruments like urine test strips, blood ketone meters, or breath analyzers to measure your ketone levels. These tools will help you determine if your body is in ketosis and enable you to change your diet if required.

**Keep a Journal:** Record your dietary consumption, exercise habits, energy levels, and any physical or mental changes. This can help you detect trends and make modifications to enhance your performance.

**Body measures:** In addition to recording your weight, take measures of your waist, hips, thighs, and arms to observe changes in body composition. Sometimes, you may drop inches even when the scale doesn't reflect considerable weight reduction.

In order to achieve success with the Hyper Ketosis Diet, it's vital to equip yourself with the appropriate tools and information. Understanding how to control your macronutrients, measure your progress, and maintain consistency in your eating habits can make the shift simpler and more successful. This section discusses the fundamental tools for success and the vital function that macronutrients—fats, proteins, and carbohydrates—play in a hyperketosis diet.

### Essential Tools for Success

Achieving and sustaining ketosis demands a certain amount of devotion and accuracy. The following tools and resources will help you keep on track, assess your progress, and make required modifications to enhance your outcomes.

### 1. Food Scale

A food scale is one of the most crucial instruments when beginning a Hyper Ketosis Diet. Accurately managing the portion sizes of your meals ensures that you are consuming the right quantities of fats, proteins, and carbohydrates.

**Why It's Important:** Portion management is crucial on a hyper ketosis diet, particularly when keeping carbohydrates low and balancing proteins and fats. Using a food scale ensures you don't underestimate or exceed your macronutrient consumption.

**How to Use It:** Weigh all your ingredients before cooking or ingesting them. This is especially crucial for high-fat foods like nuts, oils, and cheeses, which are calorie-dense and easy to overeat.

## 2. Ketone Testing Tools

Measuring ketone levels is crucial to check if your body is in ketosis and how deeply you are in this metabolic state. Several techniques are available for measuring ketone levels:

**Urine Test Strips:** These strips are affordable and commonly accessible. They quantify the quantity of ketones excreted in your urine, although they are often less accurate as your body adjusts to ketosis.

**Blood Ketone Meters:** Blood meters measure beta-hydroxybutyrate (BHB), a ketone body generated by the liver. These offer the most precise measurement of your ketone levels. However, they may be more costly, and the test strips are generally single-use.

**Breath Ketone Analyzers:** These devices test acetone levels in your breath, one of the by-products of fat breakdown during ketosis. While they are less intrusive and may be used frequently, they may not always be as exact as blood testing.

## 3. Macro-Tracking Apps

Keeping track of your daily food consumption is vital to ensure you're ingesting the correct amount of fats, proteins, and carbohydrates. Macro-tracking programs are important for this task:

**MyFitnessPal:** This popular software enables you to track meals, scan barcodes for nutritional information, and personalize your macronutrient objectives.

**Carb Manager:** Specifically built for low-carb and keto diets, Carb Manager makes it simple to log your carb consumption, assess progress, and find hundreds of keto-friendly recipes.

**Cronometer**: This app enables thorough nutrition monitoring, including vitamins, minerals, and macronutrients. It's helpful for ensuring you're reaching your nutritional requirements beyond simply fats, proteins, and carbohydrates.

## 4. Meal Prep Containers

Staying on track with a Hyper Ketosis Diet typically entails planning meals in advance. Having high-quality meal prep containers can help you keep organized and make sure you always have keto-friendly alternatives on hand.

**Why It's Important:** Preparing your meals ahead of time decreases the temptation to deviate from your diet, particularly when life becomes hectic. It also helps with portion management and ensures that you stay to your macronutrient targets.

**How to Use Them:** Cook bigger amounts of your favorite keto recipes, split them into individual servings, and store them in meal prep containers. To simplify meal planning, you can prepare meals for the week and store them in the refrigerator

### 5. Kitchen Essentials

Stock your kitchen with keto-friendly cooking utensils and materials to ease meal prep and ensure you have the proper resources on hand:

**Blender or Immersion Blender:** Essential for preparing smoothies, fat bombs, and emulsifying keto-friendly recipes.

**Spiralizer:** If you miss pasta, a spiralizer may help you produce vegetarian noodles from zucchini or other low-carb foods.

**Non-Stick Pans and Air Fryers:** Ideal for cooking dishes with minimum oil and making crispy keto-friendly snacks without excessive frying.

**Coconut Oil, Olive Oil, MCT Oil:** These are basic oils for cooking, adding to smoothies, and improving the fat content of your meals.

## Understanding Macros: Fats, Proteins, and Carbs

Macronutrients—or macros—are the core of the Hyper Ketosis Diet. By knowing the unique functions that fats, proteins, and carbs play in your diet, you may modify your meals to enhance ketosis and obtain the best outcomes.

### Fats: The Main Source of Energy

Fats are the cornerstone of the Hyper Ketosis Diet. When carbs are limited, the body resorts to using fats as its major fuel source. The liver turns lipids into ketones, which are subsequently utilized as an alternate energy source for the brain, muscles, and other tissues.

**Percentage of Daily Calories:** On a Hyper Ketosis Diet, 70-80% of your daily calories should come from fats.

**Types of Fats:**

**Saturated Fats:** These fats are stable and suitable for cooking at high temperatures. Sources include butter, ghee, coconut oil, and animal fats.

**Monounsaturated Fats:** These fats are good for your heart and can be found in foods like olive oil, avocados, and macadamia nuts

**Polyunsaturated Fats:** Essential fatty acids such as omega-3s come under this group. Include foods like fatty fish (salmon, sardines), flaxseeds, and chia seeds in your diet.

**Medium-Chain Triglycerides (MCTs):** These are a particular sort of fat that the body rapidly turns into ketones. MCT oil and coconut oil are rich in these healthy fats, making them perfect for boosting ketone generation.

**Why Fat Matters:** Fats give prolonged energy, keep you feeling full, and assist in maintaining ketosis. They also play a crucial function in hormone production and brain health.

### Proteins: The Building Blocks

Protein consumption is vital for maintaining muscular mass, mending tissues, and sustaining general health. However, with a Hyper Ketosis Diet, it's vital to ingest modest quantities of protein. Too much protein may lead to gluconeogenesis, a process where excess protein is turned into glucose, which might possibly push you out of ketosis.

**Percentage of Daily Calories:** Aim for 15-25% of your daily calories to come from protein.

### Quality Protein Sources:

Animal Proteins: Grass-fed beef, pig, poultry, eggs, and fatty fish are great sources of high-quality, complete proteins that are also rich in fats.

Plant-Based Proteins: For those pursuing a more plant-based ketogenic strategy, consume tofu, tempeh, nuts, seeds, and low-carb protein powders.

**Balancing Protein Intake:** Consuming too little protein might result in muscle loss and impaired metabolism, while too much can

interfere with ketosis. A balanced intake is crucial.

### Carbohydrates: The Macronutrient to Limit

Carbohydrates are the most limited macronutrient in the Hyper Ketosis Diet. When carb consumption is low, the body is forced to transition from utilizing glucose (sugar) as its major energy source to burning fat and creating ketones.

**Percentage of Daily Calories:** Keep carbohydrates at 5-10% of your daily calories, or 20-50 grams of net carbs per day.

**Net Carbs:** Net carbs are the total carbohydrates minus fiber. Since fiber doesn't elevate blood sugar levels or interfere with ketosis, it's removed from the overall carb amount.

### Best Low-Carb Food Choices:

**Leafy Greens:** Spinach, kale, and arugula are nutrient-dense and low in carbohydrates.

**Cruciferous Vegetables:** Broccoli, cauliflower, and Brussels sprouts are fiber-rich and low in net carbohydrates.

**Berries:** Raspberries, strawberries, and blackberries may be eaten in moderation owing to their comparatively low carbohydrate level.

**Avocados:** This fruit is strong in healthy fats and fiber, making it suitable for a ketogenic diet.

**Avoiding rich-Carb Foods:** Grains, sweets, starchy vegetables, and most fruits are excessively rich in carbohydrates and should be avoided to remain in ketosis.

## How to Avoid the "Keto Flu"

As you begin your journey into the Hyper Ketosis Diet, you may encounter a temporary phase known as the **"keto flu."** This set of symptoms is a common reaction to the significant dietary shift your body undergoes as it transitions from using carbohydrates as its primary energy source to utilizing fats and ketones. While these symptoms might be painful, they are often short-lived and can be minimized with adequate preparation and treatment.

### What is Keto Flu?

The "keto flu" refers to a group of flu-like symptoms that some persons experience after initially commencing a ketogenic diet. It happens when the body adjusts to using fat for fuel instead of carbs. Because your body has depended on glucose (produced from carbohydrates) for energy for most of your life, the metabolic transition to ketones may be a shock to the system.

### Symptoms of keto flu might include:

**Fatigue:** A general sensation of fatigue as your body adapts to fat-burning.

**Headaches:** Dehydration and electrolyte imbalances may create headaches.

**Nausea:** The dietary shift and a rapid decrease in carbs might produce moderate stomach pain.

**Dizziness and lightheadedness:** Electrolyte depletion and dehydration may cause dizziness.

**Irritation or mood swings:** As glucose levels decline, your brain may first experience the consequences, leading to irritation.

**Muscle cramps:** The loss of electrolytes like magnesium and potassium may induce muscle cramping or weakness.

**Insomnia:** Difficulty sleeping may emerge owing to variations in blood sugar and energy levels.

**Brain fog:** Reduced mental clarity and attention may occur when the brain converts to utilizing ketones for energy.

While these symptoms seem scary, they are transient and are merely a byproduct of your body's adaptation to a fat-based metabolism. Symptoms might last anywhere from a few days to a week, but with the correct methods, you can lessen both their severity and length.

### Causes of Keto Flu

The keto flu is not caused by a virus or illness but rather by a mix of physiological changes that occur when you reduce carbs. Here's what happens:

**Glycogen Depletion:** When you dramatically cut carbohydrates, your body rapidly depletes its glycogen reserves (the stored type of glucose found in your liver and muscles). Glycogen attaches to water, so when it's used up, you lose water weight swiftly. This leads to dehydration and loss of electrolytes, which contribute to many of the keto flu symptoms.

**Electrolyte Imbalance:** Along with the water loss, your kidneys expel vital electrolytes such as salt, potassium, and magnesium. This imbalance may induce muscular cramps, disorientation, and headaches.

**Switching Energy Sources:** As your body transitions from utilizing glucose to depending on ketones, it suffers an energy shortfall in the early stages of the transition, leading to weariness, cognitive fog, and irritability.

### How to Avoid the Keto Flu

Fortunately, the keto flu is not unavoidable, and even if you do suffer symptoms, there are strategies to drastically lessen its severity. With appropriate planning and methods, you can shift into ketosis with minimum difficulty.

### 1. Stay Hydrated

One of the biggest reasons individuals feel awful during the first few days of ketosis is dehydration. When you convert to a low-carb diet, your body loses more water owing to the depletion of glycogen reserves. As you lose water, you also lose vital electrolytes.

Drink Plenty of Water: Make it a point to drink at least 2.5–3 liters (or more, depending on your activity level) of water each day. This can assist restore lost fluids and lower the risk of dehydration-related symptoms.

**Electrolyte-Rich Beverages:** Consider including electrolyte-rich liquids such as bone broth or sugar-free electrolyte supplements into your diet to replace salt, potassium, and magnesium.

### 2. Replenish Electrolytes

Electrolyte imbalance is one of the primary factors in keto flu symptoms, including muscular cramps, headaches, and exhaustion. Ensuring that you are obtaining appropriate salt, potassium, and magnesium is crucial to prevent these adverse effects.

**Increase Sodium Intake:** While salt is generally limited in regular diets, the reverse is true on a ketogenic diet. As your body loses more sodium, you need to replace it. Aim to add 1-2 tablespoons of salt to your meals each day. Drinking salted water or drinking broth (which is naturally rich in sodium) may also assist in maintaining equilibrium.

**Potassium-rich foods:** Potassium is vital for muscular function and avoiding cramps. You may boost potassium by eating low-carb, potassium-rich foods such as avocados, spinach, mushrooms, and salmon. You might also try utilizing a potassium supplement under a doctor's direction.

**Magnesium for Muscle Cramps:** Magnesium plays a critical role in sustaining muscle and nerve function. Foods such as almonds, spinach, pumpkin seeds, and dark leafy greens are great sources of magnesium. Additionally, a magnesium supplement (in the form of magnesium citrate or magnesium glycinate) may assist reduce cramps and exhaustion.

## 3. Gradually Lower Carbs

Sudden and abrupt decreases in carbs may shock the system, making the keto flu more acute. Instead of rushing headlong into a rigorous ketogenic diet, try gradually reducing your carb consumption over the period of 1-2 weeks. This strategy might offer your body more time to acclimate to utilizing fat as fuel.

**How to Transition progressively:** Start by cutting off refined carbohydrates like bread, pasta, and sugar, and progressively decrease fruit and starchy vegetables. Over time, aim to consume between 20 and 50 grams of net carbohydrates daily.

## 4. Eat Enough Fat

On a Hyper Ketosis Diet, fat becomes your body's principal source of energy. However, if you don't consume enough fat in the initial stages of ketosis, your energy levels will plunge, leading to heightened sensations of exhaustion and brain fog. Make sure you're ingesting lots of high-quality fats to offer your body a constant energy source.

**Increase Your Fat Intake:** Make sure to consume enough healthy fats, such as avocados, coconut oil, olive oil, butter, fatty cuts of meat, and MCT oil. This not only feeds your body but also keeps you feeling full and content.

**Fat Bombs:** These high-fat, low-carb snacks are a wonderful way to enhance your fat consumption. You may prepare them using items like cream cheese, coconut oil, and nut butter.

## 5. Eat Enough Calories

While it might be tempting to limit calories for rapid weight reduction, doing so can actually increase keto flu symptoms. When shifting to a new energy source, your body requires appropriate calories to power this transformation.

**Don't Starve Yourself:** Ensure you're consuming enough calories to meet your body's needs. Focus on nutrient-dense, entire meals that give not just calories but also the vitamins and minerals essential for energy generation.

**Listen to Your Body:** If you feel extremely hungry or weary, it might be an indication that you're not eating enough. Tune into your body's hunger cues and ensure that you're eating enough to assist the shift to ketosis.

## 6. Supplement with MCT Oil

Medium-chain triglycerides (MCTs) are a form of fat that is readily turned into ketones by the liver, making them an ideal energy source during the transition into ketosis. Taking MCT oil supplements can help increase ketone levels quickly, reducing the fatigue and brain fog often experienced during the keto flu.

**How to Use MCT Oil:** Add MCT oil to your coffee, smoothies, or meals to enhance your fat intake and assist deliver rapid energy throughout the adaption period.

## 7. Rest and Manage Stress

The early phases of ketosis may impose stress on your body, and combining it with external stresses or inadequate rest can increase keto flu symptoms.

**Prioritize Sleep:** Aim for at least 7-9 hours of sleep every night to give your body the rest it needs to adjust to ketosis.

Stress Management: Engage in stress-relieving activities like yoga, meditation, deep breathing, or mild exercise to keep your cortisol levels in line. High cortisol may enhance weariness and irritation, making the keto flu seem worse.

## 8. Light Exercise

While strenuous exercises may not be appropriate during the first few days of your keto transition, modest exercise might help reduce the symptoms of keto flu by increasing blood circulation and boosting mood.

**Types of Exercise:** Opt for low-intensity exercises like walking, moderate yoga, or stretching during the adaption period. Avoid high-intensity interval training (HIIT) or heavy lifting, since they might drain your energy levels more while your body is adapting.

The keto flu is a transitory period that many individuals experience when they move into ketosis, but with the appropriate methods, it may be reduced or even avoided. Remember, the keto flu is a sign that your body is making the move to fat-burning mode—embrace the process, and you'll soon be enjoying the long-term advantages of sustained energy, mental clarity,

**Daily Meal Plans for Beginners (Weeks 1-2)**

When starting a Hyper Ketosis Diet, it's crucial to have a well-structured meal plan that not only supports your transition into ketosis but also ensures you're consuming the right balance of nutrients to sustain energy and prevent early challenges such as the "keto flu." During the first two weeks of this diet, your body will begin adjusting to using fats and ketones as its primary fuel source, making your choice of meals particularly important.

This section will provide a comprehensive, easy-to-follow meal plan for the first two weeks of your Hyper Ketosis journey. Each day includes breakfast, lunch, dinner, and snack options that are high in healthy fats, moderate in protein, and low in carbohydrates, designed to keep you in a state of ketosis and to support energy levels, weight loss, and overall health.

**Key Principles of the Meal Plan**

Before diving into the meal plans, it's important to understand the guiding principles behind them:

**Macronutrient Ratios:** The Hyper Ketosis Diet is characterized by a high fat intake (about 70-75% of total calories), moderate protein intake (20-25%), and very low carbohydrate intake (5-10%). These ratios help maintain ketosis by minimizing glucose production and encouraging fat burning.

**Carbohydrate Restriction:** To stay in ketosis, carbohydrate intake must be limited to around 20-50 grams of net carbs per day. This means focusing on low-carb vegetables, avoiding sugar, and steering clear of high-carb grains and starchy foods.

**Hydration and Electrolytes:** Hydration is crucial during the first weeks, as your body will shed excess water and electrolytes. Make sure to drink plenty of water and consume foods or supplements rich in sodium, potassium, and magnesium to prevent the keto flu.

**Healthy Fats:** Emphasize high-quality fats, such as those from avocados, olive oil, coconut oil, fatty fish, nuts, and seeds, to fuel your body during the metabolic shift.

# Weeks 1-2: Daily Meal Plans

## Week 1: Easing into Ketosis

During the first week, your goal is to introduce your body to the concept of ketosis by gradually lowering your carbohydrate intake while increasing fat consumption. The meal plans are designed to help you ease into this shift without overwhelming your body.

## Day 1

**Breakfast: Avocado and Bacon Omelet**

**Ingredients:** 2 large eggs, 1/2 avocado, 2 slices of bacon, 1 tbsp butter, salt, and pepper.

**Instructions:** Cook the bacon in a skillet until crispy, then set aside. In the same pan, melt butter and scramble the eggs with the avocado. Serve with crumbled bacon on top.

**Lunch: Grilled Chicken Salad with Olive Oil and Avocado**

**Ingredients:** 100g grilled chicken breast, 1 cup mixed greens, 1/2 avocado, 1 tbsp olive oil, 1 tbsp lemon juice, salt, and pepper.

**Instructions:** Mix greens and avocado in a bowl. Drizzle with olive oil and lemon juice. Top with grilled chicken.

**Dinner: Baked Salmon with Roasted Asparagus**

**Ingredients:** 150g salmon fillet, 1 tbsp olive oil, 1 tsp garlic powder, 1 bunch asparagus, salt, and pepper.

**Instructions:** Drizzle olive oil and garlic powder over salmon and asparagus. Roast at 375°F (190°C) for 15-20 minutes.

**Snacks:**

1 handful of almonds

A small serving of full-fat Greek yogurt with chia seeds

## Day 2

**Breakfast: Keto Bulletproof Coffee**

**Ingredients:** 1 cup brewed coffee, 1 tbsp MCT oil, 1 tbsp grass-fed butter.

**Instructions:** Mix all the ingredients until they're smooth and foamy.

**Lunch: Egg Salad Lettuce Wraps**

**Ingredients:** 2 hard-boiled eggs, 1 tbsp mayonnaise, 1 tbsp mustard, 4 large lettuce leaves, salt, and pepper.

**Instructions:** Mash eggs with mayonnaise and mustard. Season and scoop into lettuce leaves.

**Dinner: Beef Stir-Fry with Cauliflower Rice**

**Ingredients:** 150g grass-fed beef strips, 1 tbsp coconut oil, 1 cup cauliflower rice, 1/2 cup bell peppers, 1 tbsp soy sauce (or coconut aminos).

**Instructions:** Sauté beef in coconut oil. Stir-fry bell peppers and cauliflower rice. Add soy sauce to taste.

**Snacks:**

A few slices of cheese with cucumber

A small handful of macadamia nuts

### Day 3

**Breakfast: Keto Chia Pudding**

**Ingredients:** 1/4 cup chia seeds, 1 cup unsweetened almond milk, 1 tbsp coconut oil, 1/2 tsp vanilla extract.

**Instructions:** Mix chia seeds with almond milk and let sit overnight. Before serving, stir in coconut oil and vanilla.

**Lunch: Tuna Salad with Avocado**

**Ingredients:** 1 can of tuna, 1/2 avocado, 1 tbsp mayonnaise, 1 tbsp lemon juice, salt, and pepper.

**Instructions:** Mash avocado and mix with tuna, mayonnaise, and lemon juice. Serve on a bed of spinach.

---

**Dinner: Grilled Pork Chops with Garlic Butter**

**Ingredients:** 150g pork chop, 2 tbsp butter, 1 garlic clove (minced), salt, and pepper.

**Instructions:** Grill the pork chop and top with garlic butter before serving.

---

**Snacks:**

Celery sticks with cream cheese

Boiled egg with a sprinkle of salt

### Day 4

---

**Breakfast: Scrambled Eggs with Spinach and Feta**

**Ingredients:** 2 large eggs, 1 cup spinach, 1/4 cup feta cheese, 1 tbsp butter.

**Instructions:** Scramble eggs in butter with spinach. Top with crumbled feta.

---

**Lunch: Chicken Caesar Salad**

**Ingredients:** 100g grilled chicken, 1 cup romaine lettuce, 1 tbsp Caesar dressing, 1 tbsp Parmesan cheese, 1 tbsp olive oil.

**Instructions:** Toss lettuce with dressing, top with chicken and Parmesan.

---

**Dinner: Spiralized Zucchini with Pesto and Grilled Shrimp**

**Ingredients:** 1 zucchini (spiralized), 150g grilled shrimp, 2 tbsp pesto, salt, and pepper.

**Instructions:** Toss zucchini noodles with pesto and serve with grilled shrimp.

**Snacks:**

A handful of walnuts

Sliced bell peppers with guacamole

### Day 5

**Breakfast: Keto Pancakes with Almond Flour**

**Ingredients:** A quarter cup of almond flour, two large eggs, one tablespoon of butter, a quarter teaspoon of baking powder, and cinnamon to taste.

**Instructions:** Mix ingredients and cook on a hot skillet with butter. Top with butter or whipped cream.

**Lunch: Turkey and Avocado Lettuce Wraps**

**Ingredients:** 100g deli turkey slices, 1/2 avocado, 4 large lettuce leaves, 1 tbsp mustard.

**Instructions:** Spread avocado on turkey slices, drizzle with mustard, and wrap in lettuce.

**Dinner: Grilled Chicken Thighs with Broccoli**

**Ingredients:** 150g chicken thighs, 1 tbsp olive oil, 1 tsp paprika, 1 cup steamed broccoli.

**Instructions:** Grill chicken thighs and serve with broccoli.

**Snacks:**

Cheese and olives

Hard-boiled eggs with sea salt

## Day 6

**Breakfast: Keto Smoothie**

**Ingredients:** avocado (1/2), unsweetened almond milk (1 cup), chia seeds (1 tbsp), coconut oil (1 tbsp), ice cubes.

**Instructions:** Blend all ingredients until smooth.

**Lunch: Spinach and Bacon Salad**

**Ingredients:** 2 cups spinach, 2 slices of bacon, 1 tbsp olive oil, 1 tbsp balsamic vinegar.

**Instructions:** Cook bacon, chop it, and mix with spinach. Drizzle olive oil and balsamic vinegar on top.

**Dinner: Herb-Roasted Lamb with Cauliflower Mash**

**Ingredients:** 150g lamb chops, 1 tbsp olive oil, 1 tsp rosemary, 1 cup cauliflower (steamed and mashed).

**Instructions:** Roast lamb with rosemary and olive oil. Serve with cauliflower mash.

**Snacks:**

Almond butter on cucumber slices

Coconut flakes

## Day 7

**Breakfast: Eggs Benedict with Keto Hollandaise**

**Ingredients:** 2 large eggs, 1 slice of ham, 1 tbsp butter, 1/4 cup heavy cream, 1 tsp lemon juice.

**Instructions:** Make poached eggs and cooked ham, then drizzle them with homemade hollandaise sauce

---

**Lunch: Salmon and Cucumber Salad**

**Ingredients:** 100g smoked salmon, 1/2 cucumber (sliced), 1 tbsp olive oil, 1 tbsp lemon juice.

**Instructions:** Toss together cucumber and salmon with a dressing of olive oil and lemon juice.

---

**Dinner: Garlic Butter Steak with Green Beans**

**Ingredients:** 150g steak, 2 tbsp butter, 1 garlic clove (minced), 1 cup steamed green beans.

**Instructions:** Grill steak and top with garlic butter. Serve with green beans.

**Snacks:**

Fat bombs (made with coconut oil and cocoa powder)

Sliced avocado with sea salt

# Week 2: Deepening Ketosis

By Week 2, your body should be well on its way to adapting to the ketogenic state. During this phase, you'll continue to focus on high-fat, low-carb meals but may begin to explore more variety and new recipes. You may also notice improved energy levels, reduced cravings, and steady weight loss.

This two-week meal plan is designed to guide beginners through the early stages of the Hyper Ketosis diet, offering structure and ensuring adequate nutrition while maintaining ketosis. For lasting success, listen to your body, stay hydrated, and monitor your macronutrient intake to stay in the desired fat-burning zone.

## Week 2: Daily Meal Plans

### Day 8

**Breakfast: Keto Breakfast Casserole**

**Ingredients:** 4 large eggs, 1/4 cup shredded cheddar cheese, 1/4 cup diced bell peppers, 2 slices of bacon, 1 tbsp butter, salt, and pepper.

**Instructions:** Preheat the oven to 350°F (175°C). Cook the bacon until it's golden brown and crispy, then set it aside. In the same pan, sauté the bell peppers in butter. Whisk eggs in a bowl, add cheese, bacon, and bell peppers. Pour the mixture into a greased baking dish and bake for 20 minutes or until set.

### Lunch: Shrimp and Avocado Salad

**Ingredients:** shrimp (150g), avocado (1/2), mixed greens (1 cup), olive oil (1 tbsp), lemon juice (1 tbsp), salt, pepper.

**Instructions:** Cook shrimp and toss with mixed greens, avocado, olive oil, and lemon juice.

### Dinner: Creamy Chicken Alfredo with Zucchini Noodles

**Ingredients:** 150g chicken breast, 1 zucchini (spiralized), 1/4 cup heavy cream, 1 tbsp butter, 1 garlic clove (minced), 1 tbsp Parmesan cheese.

**Instructions:** Cook the chicken with butter, then stir in garlic and heavy cream. Simmer until thickened. Toss zucchini noodles in the sauce and sprinkle with Parmesan cheese.

### Snacks:

A handful of sunflower seeds

Cheese cubes with a few olives

### Day 9

### Breakfast: Keto Avocado Smoothie

**Ingredients:** 1/2 avocado, 1/2 cup full-fat coconut milk, 1/2 cup unsweetened almond milk, 1 tbsp MCT oil, ice cubes.

**Instructions:** Blend all ingredients until smooth.

### Lunch: Turkey and Spinach Roll-Ups

**Ingredients:** 100g deli turkey, 1 cup spinach, 2 tbsp cream cheese, 1 tbsp mustard, salt, and pepper.

**Instructions:** Create turkey pinwheels by spreading cream cheese on turkey slices and adding spinach and mustard.

---

**Dinner: Grilled Steak and Roasted Brussels with Garlic Butter**

**Ingredients:** 150g steak, 2 tbsp butter, 1 garlic clove (minced), 1 cup Brussels sprouts, salt, and pepper.

**Instructions:** Grill steak and top with garlic butter. Roast Brussels sprouts in the oven with olive oil until crispy.

---

**Snacks:**

Fat bombs made with coconut oil, cocoa powder, and almond butter

A boiled egg with mayonnaise

---

**Breakfast: Keto Scrambled Eggs with Chorizo**

**Ingredients:** 2 large eggs, 50g chorizo, 1 tbsp butter, 1/4 cup shredded cheese, salt, and pepper.

**Instructions:** Cook chorizo in a skillet. In the same pan, scramble the eggs with butter and mix in the chorizo and cheese.

---

**Lunch: Chicken Salad with Avocado and Bacon**

**Ingredients:** 100g cooked chicken breast, 1/2 avocado, 2 slices of bacon (cooked), 1 tbsp mayonnaise, salt, and pepper.

**Instructions:** Chop chicken, avocado, and bacon. Toss with mayonnaise and serve over a bed of lettuce.

**Dinner: Lemon Butter Salmon with Cauliflower Rice**

**Ingredients:** 150g salmon fillet, 1 tbsp butter, 1 tbsp lemon juice, 1 cup cauliflower rice, salt, and pepper.

**Instructions:** Sauté the salmon in butter and drizzle with lemon juice. Serve with cauliflower rice.

---

**Snacks:**

A few slices of salami with cheese

A variety of mixed nuts, including almonds, walnuts, and macadamias.

**Breakfast: Keto Breakfast Muffins**

**Ingredients:** 4 large eggs, 1/4 cup cheddar cheese, 1/4 cup diced ham, 1/4 cup diced bell peppers, salt, and pepper.

**Instructions:** Preheat the oven to 350°F (175°C). Whisk the eggs, then stir in ham, cheese, and bell peppers. Pour into a greased muffin tin and bake for 15-20 minutes.

---

**Lunch: Tuna Salad Stuffed Avocados**

**Ingredients:** 1 can of tuna, 1/2 avocado, 1 tbsp mayonnaise, 1 tbsp lemon juice, salt, and pepper.

**Instructions:** Mix tuna with mayonnaise and lemon juice. Scoop the mixture into halved avocados.

**Dinner: Grilled Chicken Thighs with Garlic Butter and Broccoli**

**Ingredients:** 150g chicken thighs, 2 tbsp butter, 1 garlic clove (minced), 1 cup steamed broccoli, salt, and pepper.

**Instructions:** Grill chicken thighs and top with garlic butter. Serve with steamed broccoli.

---

**Snacks:**

Celery sticks with almond butter

Hard-boiled eggs with sea salt

### Day 12

**Breakfast: Keto Smoothie Bowl**

**Ingredients:** 1/2 avocado, 1/2 cup full-fat coconut milk, 1 tbsp chia seeds, 1 tbsp coconut oil, 1/4 cup mixed berries (optional).

**Instructions:** Blend the avocado, coconut milk, chia seeds, and coconut oil. Top with a few mixed berries for added texture.

---

**Lunch: Egg and Bacon Salad**

**Ingredients:** hard-boiled eggs (2), bacon (2 slices), spinach (1 cup), olive oil (1 tbsp), balsamic vinegar (1 tbsp).

**Instructions:** Chop the eggs and bacon. Mix with spinach, olive oil, and balsamic vinegar.

---

**Dinner: Herb-Crusted Pork Chops with Roasted Zucchini**

**Ingredients:** pork chops (150g), olive oil (1 tbsp), rosemary (1 tbsp), zucchini (1), salt, pepper.

**Instructions:** Coat pork chops in olive oil and rosemary, then roast with zucchini slices in the oven at 375°F (190°C) for 20-25 minutes.

---

**Snacks:**

A handful of macadamia nuts

Cheese with cucumber slices

## Day 13

### Breakfast: Keto Egg Muffins with Spinach and Cheese

**Ingredients:** 4 large eggs, 1 cup spinach, 1/4 cup shredded cheese, 1 tbsp butter, salt, and pepper.

**Instructions:** Whisk the eggs and stir in spinach and cheese. Pour into greased muffin tins and bake at 350°F (175°C) for 15-20 minutes.

### Lunch: Grilled Chicken Caesar Salad

**Ingredients:** 100g grilled chicken, 2 cups romaine lettuce, 2 tbsp Caesar dressing, 1 tbsp Parmesan cheese.

**Instructions:** Toss the lettuce with Caesar dressing and top with grilled chicken and Parmesan.

### Dinner: Garlic Shrimp with Zucchini Noodles

**Ingredients:** 150g shrimp, 1 zucchini (spiralized), 1 tbsp butter, 1 garlic clove (minced), salt, and pepper.

**Instructions:** Cook shrimp in butter and garlic. Combine the zucchini noodles with the shrimp mixture.

### Snacks:

A small handful of almonds

Almond flour (1/4 cup), large eggs (2), butter (1 tbsp), baking powder (1/4 tsp), cinnamon (to taste)

## Day 14

**Breakfast: Keto Waffles with Almond Flour**

**Ingredients:** 1/4 cup almond flour, 2 large eggs, 1 tbsp butter, 1/4 tsp baking powder, cinnamon to taste.

**Instructions:** Mix the ingredients and cook in a waffle maker. Top with butter or whipped cream.

**Lunch: Egg Salad Lettuce Wraps**

**Ingredients:** Two hard-boiled eggs, one tablespoon of mayonnaise, one tablespoon of mustard, four large lettuce leaves, and salt and pepper.

**Instructions:** Mash the eggs with mayonnaise and mustard. Scoop the mixture into lettuce leaves and wrap.

**Dinner: Lemon Herb Chicken with Cauliflower Mash**

**Ingredients:** 150g chicken breast, 1 tbsp olive oil, 1 tbsp lemon juice, 1 cup cauliflower (steamed and mashed), salt, and pepper.

**Instructions:** Grill the chicken with olive oil and lemon juice. Serve with cauliflower mash.

**Snacks:**

Cheese cubes with olives

Celery with cream cheese

## Transitioning into Week 3

By the end of Week 2, your body should be well-adapted to ketosis, burning fat for fuel efficiently. You might notice increased energy, mental clarity, and possibly weight loss. As you transition into Week 3, you'll have more flexibility in your food choices, though the focus remains on maintaining the high-fat, low-carb, moderate-protein principles that define the Hyper Ketosis Diet. Keep tracking your macros, staying hydrated, and ensuring that your meals are nutrient-dense to continue reaping the benefits of ketosis.

## Intermediate Meal Plans (Weeks 3-4)

As you move into Weeks 3 and 4 of the Hyper Ketosis diet, your body should have fully adapted to using fat as its primary fuel source. This phase builds upon the foundation laid in the first two weeks, allowing for more flexibility in your meal planning while still adhering to the high-fat, low-carb structure that keeps your body in ketosis. You may notice improved energy, enhanced mental clarity, better physical performance, and more significant fat loss. This phase also encourages you to explore more varied ingredients and recipes.

## Week 3: Enhancing Ketosis

In Week 3, you'll focus on deepening your state of ketosis by continuing to limit carbohydrates to under 20-25 grams per day while increasing healthy fats. By now, you may be experimenting with new recipes and expanding your ingredient list to avoid monotony. The goal is to maintain ketosis while keeping meals interesting and satisfying.

## Day 15

### Breakfast: Keto Breakfast Burrito (with a Low-Carb Tortilla)

**Ingredients:** 2 large eggs, 1/4 cup shredded cheddar cheese, 2 slices of bacon, 1 low-carb tortilla, 1 tbsp sour cream, salt, and pepper.

**Instructions:** Scramble eggs with cheese, cook bacon, and wrap both in the low-carb tortilla. Top with sour cream and serve.

### Lunch: Grilled Salmon Salad

**Ingredients:** 150g grilled salmon, 2 cups mixed greens, 1 tbsp olive oil, 1 tbsp lemon juice, 1 tbsp avocado slices, salt, and pepper.

**Instructions:** Grill salmon and serve over mixed greens with olive oil and lemon dressing.

### Dinner: Keto Beef Stir-Fry

**Ingredients:** Beef strips (150g), broccoli florets (1 cup), bell pepper (sliced), soy sauce (1 tbsp), coconut oil (1 tbsp)

**Instructions:** Stir-fry the beef in coconut oil until browned. Add broccoli and bell pepper. Season with soy sauce and sauté until vegetables are tender.

### Snacks:

Keto-friendly beef jerky

A small handful of walnuts

## Day 16

**Breakfast: Coconut Flour Pancakes with Butter and Berries**

**Ingredients:** 1/4 cup coconut flour, 2 large eggs, 1/4 cup unsweetened almond milk, 1 tbsp butter, a few berries for garnish.

**Instructions:** Whisk ingredients and cook like regular pancakes in butter. Serve with additional butter and some berries.

**Lunch: Eggplant and Mozzarella Bake**

**Ingredients:** 1 large eggplant (sliced), 1/2 cup mozzarella cheese, 1/4 cup marinara sauce (low-carb), 1 tbsp olive oil, basil for garnish.

**Instructions:** Grill eggplant slices and layer with marinara sauce and cheese. Bake until the cheese is melted and has a bubbly appearance.

**Dinner: Lemon Herb Chicken Thighs with Cauliflower Rice**

**Ingredients:** 150g chicken thighs, 1 cup cauliflower rice, 1 tbsp olive oil, 1 tbsp lemon juice, garlic powder, salt, and pepper.

**Instructions:** Grill chicken thighs marinated in olive oil and lemon juice. Serve with cauliflower rice seasoned with garlic powder.

**Snacks:**

Celery sticks with almond butter

A boiled egg with sea salt

## Day 17

**Breakfast: Avocado and Bacon Omelet**

**Ingredients:** 3 large eggs, 1/2 avocado (sliced), 2 slices of bacon (cooked), 1 tbsp butter, salt, and pepper.

**Instructions:** Whisk eggs and cook in butter, then fold in avocado and bacon before serving.

**Lunch: Greek Salad with Feta and Olives**

**Ingredients:** 1 cup cucumbers (chopped), 1 cup tomatoes (chopped), 1/4 cup feta cheese, 1/4 cup Kalamata olives, 1 tbsp olive oil, 1 tbsp red wine vinegar.

**Instructions:** Toss all ingredients in olive oil and vinegar, season with salt and pepper.

**Dinner: Garlic Butter Shrimp with Zoodles**

**Ingredients:** 150g shrimp, 2 zucchini (spiralized), 2 tbsp butter, 1 garlic clove (minced), salt, and pepper.

**Instructions:** Sauté shrimp in garlic butter and toss with zucchini noodles. Serve hot.

**Snacks:**

Sliced avocado with sea salt

Cheese and olives

**Day 18**

**Breakfast: Keto Chia Pudding with Almond Butter**

**Ingredients:** Chia seeds (1/4 cup), unsweetened almond milk (1/2 cup), almond butter (1 tbsp), vanilla extract (1/4 tsp)

**Instructions:** Combine chia seeds with almond milk and vanilla, let sit overnight. Top with almond butter before serving.

**Lunch: Keto Chicken Caesar Wrap**

**Ingredients:** 100g grilled chicken, 1 low-carb tortilla, 2 tbsp Caesar dressing, 1/4 cup Parmesan cheese, 1/2 cup romaine lettuce.

**Instructions:** Assemble wrap with chicken, lettuce, dressing, and cheese.

**Dinner: Keto Meatballs with Zoodles**

**Ingredients:** 150g ground beef, 1 egg, 1 tbsp Parmesan cheese, 1 zucchini (spiralized), 1/4 cup marinara sauce (low-carb).

**Instructions:** Mix ground beef with egg and cheese, shape into meatballs, and bake. Top with zucchini noodles and marinara sauce.

**Snacks:**

A small handful of macadamia nuts

Sliced cucumber with guacamole

## Day 19

### Breakfast: Bulletproof Coffee

**Ingredients:** 1 cup brewed coffee, 1 tbsp butter, 1 tbsp MCT oil, 1 tbsp heavy cream.

**Instructions:** Blend all ingredients together for a creamy, high-fat coffee to start your day.

### Lunch: Tuna-Stuffed Bell Peppers

**Ingredients:** 1 can of tuna, 2 bell peppers (halved), 1 tbsp mayonnaise, salt, and pepper.

**Instructions:** Season tuna with salt and pepper, then mix with mayonnaise. Stuff into bell pepper halves and serve.

### Dinner: Herb-Crusted Pork Loin with Roasted Vegetables

**Ingredients**: 150g pork loin, 1 tbsp olive oil, rosemary, thyme, salt, and pepper, 1 cup mixed vegetables (broccoli, cauliflower).

**Instructions:** Coat pork loin with olive oil and herbs, roast alongside vegetables at 375°F (190°C) for 20-25 minutes.

**Snacks:**

Boiled eggs with sea salt

Almond butter with celery sticks

## Day 20

### Breakfast: Keto Egg Muffins with Bacon and Cheese

**Ingredients:** 4 large eggs, 2 slices of bacon (cooked and crumbled), 1/4 cup shredded cheese, salt, and pepper.

**Instructions:** Whisk eggs and mix in bacon and cheese. Pour into muffin tins and bake at 350°F (175°C) for 15 minutes.

### Lunch: Spinach and Feta Salad with Walnuts

**Ingredients:** Spinach (2 cups), feta cheese (1/4 cup), walnuts (1/4 cup), olive oil (1 tbsp), balsamic vinegar (1 tbsp)

**Instructions:** Toss all ingredients in olive oil and balsamic vinegar.

### Dinner: Keto Shepherd's Pie with Cauliflower Mash

**Ingredients:** 150g ground beef, 1 cup cauliflower (steamed and mashed), 1/4 cup cheddar cheese, salt, and pepper.

**Instructions:** Brown the beef, season with salt and pepper. Layer the ingredients, top with cauliflower mash and cheese, and bake at 375°F (190°C) until the cheese is melted.

**Snacks:**

A few slices of salami with cheese

Sliced avocado with olive oil

## Week 4: Fine-Tuning Ketosis

As you reach Week 4, you're fine-tuning your diet to keep yourself in a consistent state of ketosis. At this stage, many people experience more stable weight loss, improved physical performance, and fewer hunger pangs. Your meal plans may begin to reflect more personal preferences, allowing for a greater variety of keto-friendly foods. You'll continue to track macros and stay hydrated while exploring new recipes to avoid boredom.

### Day 21

**Breakfast: Keto Scrambled Eggs with Spinach and Feta**

**Ingredients:** 3 large eggs, 1/4 cup feta cheese, 1 cup spinach, 1 tbsp butter, salt, and pepper.

**Instructions:** Sauté spinach in butter, then scramble eggs and mix in feta.

**Lunch: Turkey and Avocado Salad**

**Ingredients:** 100g cooked turkey, 1/2 avocado (sliced), 1 cup mixed greens, 1 tbsp olive oil, 1 tbsp lemon juice.

**Instructions:** Toss all ingredients in olive oil and lemon juice.

**Dinner: Keto Alfredo with Zoodles**

**Ingredients:** 150g chicken, 2 zucchini (spiralized), 1/4 cup heavy cream, 1/4 cup Parmesan cheese, 1 garlic clove (minced).

**Instructions:** Cook chicken and garlic in butter. Add cream and Parmesan, and toss with zucchini noodles.

### Day 22

**Breakfast: Keto Avocado and Bacon Egg Cups**

**Ingredients:** 1 avocado (halved and pitted), 2 large eggs, 2 slices bacon (cooked and crumbled), salt, and pepper.

**Instructions:** Preheat oven to 375°F (190°C). Scoop out a bit of avocado to create space. Place avocado halves in a baking dish. Crack an egg into each half, sprinkle with bacon, salt, and pepper. Bake for 15-20 minutes.

**Lunch: Keto Greek Salad with Grilled Chicken**

**Ingredients:** 150g grilled chicken breast, 2 cups mixed greens, 1/4 cup sliced cucumbers, 1/4 cup sliced olives, 1/4 cup feta cheese, 1 tbsp olive oil, 1 tbsp red wine vinegar.

**Instructions:** Combine greens with cucumbers, olives, feta, and grilled chicken. Drizzle with olive oil and red wine vinegar, and enjoy.

**Dinner: Keto Beef Stroganoff with Shirataki Noodles**

**Ingredients:** 150g beef strips, 1 cup mushrooms (sliced), 1/4 cup heavy cream, 2 tbsp olive oil, 1 garlic clove (minced), 1 package Shirataki noodles, salt, and pepper.

**Instructions:** Cook beef and garlic in olive oil. Add mushrooms and cook until tender. Stir in heavy cream and season. Serve over Shirataki noodles.

**Snacks:**

1 oz of mixed nuts

A few slices of cucumber with hummus

**Breakfast: Keto Protein Pancakes with Blueberries**

**Ingredients:** 1/2 cup almond flour, 1/4 cup protein powder, 2 large eggs, 1/4 cup unsweetened almond milk, 1/2 cup blueberries, 1 tbsp butter.

**Instructions:** Mix all ingredients and cook pancakes on a griddle over medium heat. Top with blueberries.

**Lunch: Keto Stuffed Bell Peppers**

**Ingredients:** Bell peppers (2), ground turkey (150g), shredded cheese (1/4 cup), diced tomatoes (1/4 cup), olive oil (1 tbsp), salt, pepper

**Instructions:** Preheat oven to 375°F (190°C). Cook ground turkey with tomatoes, salt, and pepper. Stuff bell peppers with turkey mixture, top with cheese, and bake for 25 minutes.

**Dinner: Keto Shrimp and Broccoli Stir-Fry**

**Ingredients:** 150g shrimp, 1 cup broccoli florets, 2 tbsp coconut oil, 1 tbsp soy sauce (low-carb), 1 garlic clove (minced), salt, and pepper.

**Instructions:** Stir-fry shrimp and garlic in coconut oil. Add broccoli and soy sauce, cook until broccoli is tender.

**Snacks:**

A handful of walnuts

Keto coconut fat bombs

## Day 24

### Breakfast: Keto Egg and Spinach Breakfast Bake

**Ingredients:** 4 large eggs, 1 cup fresh spinach, 1/4 cup shredded mozzarella cheese, 1 tbsp olive oil, salt, and pepper.

**Instructions:** Preheat oven to 375°F (190°C). Whisk eggs and mix with spinach and cheese. Pour into a greased baking dish and bake for 25 minutes.

### Lunch: Keto Chicken Caesar Salad

**Ingredients:** 150g grilled chicken breast, 2 cups romaine lettuce, 1/4 cup Parmesan cheese, 2 tbsp Caesar dressing (low-carb).

**Instructions:** Toss romaine with grilled chicken, Parmesan cheese, and Caesar dressing.

### Dinner: Keto Baked Cod with Herb Butter

**Ingredients:** 150g cod fillet, 2 tbsp butter, 1 tbsp lemon juice, 1 tsp dried herbs (such as dill or thyme), salt, and pepper.

**Instructions:** Preheat oven to 400°F (200°C). Mix butter with lemon juice and herbs. Spread over cod and bake for 15-20 minutes.

**Snacks:**

A few slices of bell pepper topped with guacamole

1 oz of cheese cubes

## Day 25

### Breakfast: Keto Smoothie with Avocado and Spinach

**Ingredients:** 1/2 avocado, 1 cup unsweetened almond milk, 1 cup spinach, 1 tbsp chia seeds, 1 tbsp MCT oil.

**Instructions:** Blend all ingredients until smooth.

### Lunch: Keto Beef and Cabbage Stir-Fry

**Ingredients:** 150g beef strips, 1 cup shredded cabbage, 2 tbsp olive oil, 1 tbsp soy sauce (low-carb), 1 garlic clove (minced), salt, and pepper.

**Instructions:** Stir-fry beef and garlic in olive oil. Add cabbage and soy sauce, cook until cabbage is tender.

### Dinner: Keto Chicken Thighs with Roasted Brussels Sprouts

**Ingredients:** 150g chicken thighs, 1 cup Brussels sprouts, 2 tbsp olive oil, 1 tsp smoked paprika, salt, and pepper.

**Instructions:** Preheat oven to 400°F (200°C). Season chicken thighs and Brussels sprouts with olive oil, paprika, salt, and pepper. Roast for 25-30 minutes.

**Snacks:**

A handful of sunflower seeds

Keto-friendly chocolate mousse

**Snacks:**

A few olives

Sliced radishes with cream cheese

## Day 27

**Breakfast: Keto Egg and Sausage Breakfast Bowl**

**Ingredients:** Large eggs (2), cooked sausage (100g), avocado (sliced, 1/2), olive oil (1 tbsp), salt, pepper

**Instructions:** Cook sausage in olive oil. Scramble the eggs, then mix with the sausage and avocado slices.

## Day 26

**Breakfast: Keto Almond Flour Muffins with Berries**

**Ingredients:** 1 cup almond flour, 2 large eggs, 1/4 cup unsweetened almond milk, 1/2 cup mixed berries, 1 tsp baking powder.

**Instructions:** Mix all ingredients and bake at 350°F (175°C) for 15-20 minutes. Serve with butter.

**Lunch: Keto Chicken and Avocado Salad**

**Ingredients:** 150g cooked chicken breast (diced), 1/2 avocado (cubed), 2 cups mixed greens, 1 tbsp olive oil, 1 tbsp lemon juice.

**Instructions:** Toss chicken and avocado with mixed greens, olive oil, and lemon juice.

**Dinner: Keto Salmon with Garlic Herb Butter**

**Ingredients:** 150g salmon fillet, 2 tbsp butter, 1 garlic clove (minced), 1 tbsp chopped fresh herbs (such as parsley or dill), salt, and pepper.

**Instructions:** Cook salmon in butter with garlic and herbs. Drizzle with olive oil and red wine vinegar, and enjoy.

**Lunch: Keto Spinach and Feta Stuffed Mushrooms**

**Ingredients:** 4 large mushrooms, 1/2 cup fresh spinach (chopped), 1/4 cup crumbled feta cheese, 1 tbsp olive oil, salt, and pepper.

**Instructions:** Preheat oven to 375°F (190°C). Stuff mushrooms with spinach and feta. Drizzle with olive oil and bake for 20 minutes.

**Dinner: Keto Pork Chops with Creamy Mustard Sauce**

**Ingredients:** 150g pork chops, 2 tbsp heavy cream, 1 tbsp Dijon mustard, 1 tbsp olive oil, salt, and pepper.

**Instructions:** Cook pork chops in olive oil. Mix heavy cream and mustard for sauce and pour over pork chops.

**Snacks:**

A handful of pecans

Keto chocolate-covered almonds

### Day 28

**Breakfast: Keto Coconut Flour Pancakes**

**Ingredients:** Coconut flour (1/2 cup), large eggs (2), unsweetened almond milk (1/4 cup), baking powder (1 tsp), vanilla extract (1 tsp)

**Instructions:** Mix all ingredients and cook pancakes on a griddle over medium heat. Serve with butter or sugar-free syrup.

**Lunch: Keto Tuna Salad Lettuce Wraps**

**Ingredients**: 1 can tuna, 2 tbsp mayonnaise, 1 tbsp Dijon mustard, 1 tbsp chopped celery, large lettuce leaves.

**Instructions:** Mix tuna with mayonnaise, mustard, and celery. Spoon the mixture into lettuce leaves and wrap.

**Dinner: Keto Chicken Alfredo with Zucchini Noodles**

**Ingredients:** Chicken breast (150g), spiralized zucchini (2), heavy cream (1/4 cup), Parmesan cheese (1/4 cup), minced garlic clove (1)

**Instructions:** Sauté chicken and garlic in butter, add a creamy sauce with Parmesan, and toss with zucchini noodles.

**Snacks:**

A handful of macadamia nuts

Keto-friendly Greek yogurt with cinnamon

In Weeks 3 and 4, your focus should be on reinforcing your understanding of how to balance your meals within the Hyper Ketosis framework. Continue to adapt your meals to your preferences and nutritional needs, ensuring that you stay within your macro targets while enjoying a variety of flavors and textures.

## Advanced Meal Plans (Weeks 5-6)

As you move beyond the initial adaptation phase, Weeks 5 and 6 of the Hyper Ketosis diet offer more advanced meal plans. At this stage, your body has fully transitioned to using fat as its primary fuel source, allowing for greater flexibility in your meals. You'll be able to incorporate a wider variety of keto-friendly ingredients and fine-tune your macros based on your personal goals, whether you're aiming for fat loss, muscle gain, or maintaining ketosis for cognitive and health benefits.

The focus here is on maintaining ketosis with nutrient-dense, flavorful meals while continuing to keep carbohydrates low and healthy fats high. By this point, your understanding of macros and portion control will be well-established, allowing for easier customization of meals based on your preferences and daily routine.

## Week 5: Optimizing Fat Intake

In Week 5, you'll aim to optimize your fat intake to support sustained energy levels and continued fat-burning. By incorporating a variety of healthy fats, such as avocado, olive oil, coconut oil, and fatty cuts of meat, you'll ensure that your meals are not only keto-friendly but also enjoyable and filling.

### Day 29

**Breakfast: Keto Breakfast Bowl with Avocado and Bacon**

**Ingredients:** 2 large eggs (poached), 1/2 avocado (sliced), 2 slices of bacon (cooked), 1 tbsp olive oil, salt, and pepper.

**Instructions:** Assemble all ingredients in a bowl. Once you've added salt and pepper and drizzled with olive oil, serve.

**Lunch: Keto BLT Salad with Mayo Dressing**

**Ingredients:** 2 cups lettuce, 4 slices bacon (cooked and crumbled), 1/2 tomato (diced), 1 tbsp mayonnaise, 1 tbsp apple cider vinegar.

**Instructions:** Toss salad with bacon and tomato. Mix mayonnaise and apple cider vinegar for the dressing.

**Dinner: Keto Pork Chops with Creamy Spinach**

**Ingredients:** 150g pork chop, 1 cup spinach, 2 tbsp heavy cream, 1 tbsp butter, salt, and pepper.

**Instructions:** Cook pork chop in butter, then sauté spinach in the same pan. Add cream and cook until thickened. Serve pork chops with the creamy spinach.

**Snacks:**

1 oz cheese cubes

Macadamia nuts

## Day 30

**Breakfast: Keto Smoothie with Coconut Milk and Berries**

**Ingredients:** 1/2 cup unsweetened coconut milk, 1/4 cup mixed berries (frozen), 1 tbsp MCT oil, 1 tbsp chia seeds, 1/4 cup spinach.

**Instructions:** Mix all ingredients together, blend211 until they're smooth and creamy.

**Lunch: Tuna Salad Lettuce Wraps**

**Ingredients:** 1 can of tuna, 1 tbsp mayonnaise, 1 tbsp Dijon mustard, 1 tbsp chopped celery, 1 tbsp pickles (chopped), large lettuce leaves.

**Instructions:** Mix tuna with mayonnaise, mustard, celery, and pickles. Spoon the mixture into lettuce leaves and wrap.

**Dinner: Keto Chicken Thighs with Roasted Brussels Sprouts**

**Ingredients:** 150g chicken thighs, 1 cup Brussels sprouts, 1 tbsp olive oil, garlic powder, salt, and pepper.

**Instructions:** Roast chicken thighs and Brussels sprouts together on a sheet pan. Drizzle with olive oil, season with garlic powder, and bake at 375°F (190°C) for 20-25 minutes.

**Snacks:**

Olives with feta cheese

Boiled egg with sea salt

## Day 31

**Breakfast: Keto Bagel with Cream Cheese and Smoked Salmon**

**Ingredients:** 1 keto bagel (almond flour-based), 2 tbsp cream cheese, 50g smoked salmon, capers, and lemon slices for garnish.

**Instructions:** Toast the keto bagel, spread cream cheese, top with smoked salmon, and garnish with capers and lemon slices.

**Lunch: Keto Turkey Avocado Bowl**

**Ingredients:** 100g turkey breast (cooked), 1/2 avocado (sliced), 1 cup mixed greens, 1 tbsp olive oil, 1 tbsp balsamic vinegar.

**Instructions:** Assemble all ingredients in a bowl, drizzle with olive oil and balsamic vinegar.

**Dinner: Keto Beef Stroganoff with Zucchini Noodles**

**Ingredients:** 150g ground beef, 1/4 cup sour cream, 1 garlic clove (minced), 2 zucchini (spiralized), 1 tbsp butter, salt, and pepper.

**Instructions:** Cook beef and garlic in butter. Stir in sour cream and simmer. Serve over zucchini noodles.

**Snacks:**

Almond butter with celery sticks

Keto fat bombs (coconut oil, cacao, and almond butter)

## Day 32

**Breakfast:** **Keto Scramble with Mushrooms and Sausage**

**Ingredients:** 2 large eggs, 50g sausage (crumbled), 1/4 cup mushrooms (sliced), 1 tbsp butter, salt, and pepper.

**Instructions:** Sauté sausage and mushrooms in butter. Scramble eggs and cook together. Season with salt and pepper.

**Lunch: Keto Cobb Salad**

**Ingredients:** 2 cups romaine lettuce, 1 boiled egg (sliced), 1/2 avocado (sliced), 1/4 cup blue cheese crumbles, 2 slices of bacon (cooked and crumbled), 1 tbsp olive oil, 1 tbsp lemon juice.

**Instructions:** Make a flavorful meal: Combine all ingredients, drizzle with olive oil and lemon juice, and enjoy.

**Dinner: Keto Shrimp Scampi with Zoodles**

**Ingredients:** 150g shrimp, 2 zucchini (spiralized), 2 tbsp butter, 1 garlic clove (minced), 1 tbsp lemon juice, salt, and pepper.

**Instructions:** Sauté shrimp in butter with garlic and lemon juice. Toss with zucchini noodles and serve.

**Snacks:**

Pecans with cream cheese

Keto chia pudding with coconut milk

## Day 33

**Breakfast:** **Keto Chocolate Avocado Smoothie**

**Ingredients:** 1/2 avocado, 1 tbsp unsweetened cocoa powder, 1/2 cup unsweetened almond milk, 1 tbsp MCT oil, 1 tbsp chia seeds.

**Instructions:** Mix and blend all ingredients together until they're smooth and creamy.

**Lunch: Grilled Chicken with Caesar Salad**

**Ingredients:** 150g grilled chicken breast, 2 cups romaine lettuce, 1 tbsp Parmesan cheese, 1 tbsp Caesar dressing (low-carb).

**Instructions:** Slice grilled chicken and serve over romaine lettuce with dressing and Parmesan cheese.

**Dinner: Keto Pesto Chicken with Zoodles**

**Ingredients:** 150g chicken breast, 2 tbsp pesto (low-carb), 2 zucchini (spiralized), 1 tbsp olive oil, salt, and pepper.

**Instructions:** Cook chicken in olive oil, toss with pesto, and serve over zucchini noodles.

---

**Snacks:**

A handful of walnuts

Boiled egg with sea salt

### Day 34

**Breakfast: Keto Almond Flour Muffins with Butter**

**Ingredients:** Almond flour (1/4 cup), large eggs (2), butter (1 tbsp), baking powder (1/4 tsp), vanilla extract (1/4 tsp)

**Instructions:** Mix all ingredients and bake at 350°F (175°C) for 15-20 minutes. Serve with butter.

---

**Lunch: Keto Salmon Salad with Avocado**

**Ingredients:** 150g grilled salmon, 1/2 avocado (sliced), 2 cups spinach, 1 tbsp olive oil, 1 tbsp lemon juice.

**Instructions:** Assemble ingredients in a salad bowl, drizzle with olive oil and lemon juice.

---

**Dinner: Keto Pork Tenderloin with Creamed Spinach**

**Ingredients:** 150g pork tenderloin, 1 cup spinach, 2 tbsp heavy cream, 1 tbsp butter, salt, and pepper.

**Instructions:** Grill pork tenderloin and serve over creamed spinach (cooked in butter and heavy cream).

---

**Snacks:**

Cheese and olives

Keto trail mix (nuts, seeds, and unsweetened coconut flakes)

### Day 35

**Breakfast: Keto Greek Yogurt with Chia Seeds and Berries**

**Ingredients:** 1/2 cup full-fat Greek yogurt, 1 tbsp chia seeds, 1/4 cup mixed berries, 1 tsp vanilla extract.

**Instructions:** Create a flavorful yogurt: Mix chia seeds and vanilla extract into the yogurt. Top with berries and enjoy.

---

**Lunch: Turkey Lettuce Wraps with Avocado and Bacon**

**Ingredients**: 100g turkey breast (sliced), 1/2 avocado (sliced), 2 slices of bacon (cooked), large lettuce leaves.

**Instructions:** Assemble turkey, avocado, and bacon into lettuce leaves and wrap.

**Dinner: Keto Chicken Thighs with Garlic Butter Asparagus**

**Ingredients:** 150g chicken thighs, 1 cup asparagus, 2 tbsp butter, 1 garlic clove (minced), salt, and pepper.

**Instructions:** Cook chicken thighs in butter with garlic. Serve with sautéed asparagus.

---

**Snacks:**

Pork rinds with guacamole

Keto chocolate fat bombs

## Week 6: Maintaining Ketosis and Reaching Your Goals

By the end of Week 6, you'll have gained a comprehensive understanding of the Hyper Ketosis diet, mastered meal prep, and developed the confidence to continue your ketogenic journey.

### Day 36

**Breakfast: Keto Egg Muffins with Spinach and Cheese**

**Ingredients:** 4 large eggs, 1/2 cup spinach (chopped), 1/4 cup shredded cheddar cheese, 1/4 cup diced bell peppers, 1 tbsp olive oil, salt, and pepper.

**Instructions:** Preheat oven to 375°F (190°C). Whisk eggs, then mix in spinach, cheese, and bell peppers. Pour the batter into a greased muffin tin and bake for 20 minutes.

---

**Lunch: Keto Chicken Caesar Salad**

**Ingredients:** 150g grilled chicken breast, 2 cups romaine lettuce, 1/4 cup Parmesan cheese, 2 tbsp Caesar dressing (low-carb).

**Instructions:** Slice grilled chicken and toss with lettuce, Parmesan, and Caesar dressing.

---

**Dinner: Keto Beef and Broccoli Stir-Fry**

**Ingredients:** 150g beef strips, 1 cup broccoli florets, 2 tbsp coconut oil, 2 tbsp tamari (low-carb), 1 garlic clove (minced), salt, and pepper.

**Instructions:** Stir-fry beef and garlic in coconut oil. Add broccoli and tamari, and cook until tender.

---

**Snacks:**

1 oz of pumpkin seeds

Celery sticks with almond butter

## Day 37

**Breakfast: Keto Chia Seed Pudding with Coconut Milk**

**Ingredients:** One-fourth cup chia seeds, one-half cup unsweetened coconut milk, one tablespoon of unsweetened cocoa powder and vanilla extract each, and a few raspberries for topping.

**Instructions:** Mix chia seeds with coconut milk, cocoa powder, and vanilla extract. Refrigerate overnight and top with raspberries before serving.

**Lunch: Keto Turkey and Avocado Salad**

**Ingredients:** 100g sliced turkey breast, 1/2 avocado (diced), 2 cups mixed greens, 1 tbsp olive oil, 1 tbsp red wine vinegar.

**Instructions:** Toss turkey, avocado, and mixed greens with olive oil and red wine vinegar.

**Dinner: Keto Salmon with Lemon-Dill Sauce**

**Ingredients:** 150g salmon fillet, 2 tbsp heavy cream, 1 tbsp lemon juice, 1 tbsp fresh dill (chopped), 1 tbsp olive oil.

**Instructions:** Cook salmon in olive oil. Create a sauce and drizzle: Mix heavy cream, lemon juice, and dill to create a sauce, then pour it over the salmon.

**Snacks:**

Hard-boiled eggs

A handful of almonds

## Day 38

**Breakfast: Keto Avocado Smoothie**

**Ingredients:** 1/2 avocado, 1 cup unsweetened almond milk, 1 tbsp MCT oil, 1 tbsp flaxseeds, a few strawberries (optional).

**Instructions:** Combine all ingredients and stir until well combined and creamy.

**Lunch: Keto Chicken Salad with Mayo**

**Ingredients:** 150g cooked chicken (shredded), 2 tbsp mayonnaise, 1 tbsp chopped celery, 1 tbsp chopped pickles, salt, and pepper.

**Instructions:** Mix chicken with mayonnaise, celery, and pickles. Season with salt and pepper.

**Dinner: Keto Stuffed Bell Peppers**

**Ingredients:** 2 bell peppers, 150g ground beef, 1/4 cup shredded cheese, 1/4 cup diced tomatoes, 1 tbsp olive oil, salt, and pepper.

**Instructions:** Preheat oven to 375°F (190°C). Cook beef with tomatoes, salt, and pepper. Stuff peppers with beef mixture and top with cheese. Bake for 25 minutes.

**Snacks:**

Sliced cucumbers with guacamole

A few macadamia nuts

## Day 39

**Breakfast: Keto Almond Flour Pancakes**

**Ingredients:** 1 cup almond flour, 2 large eggs, 1/4 cup unsweetened almond milk, 1 tsp baking powder, 1 tsp vanilla extract.

Instructions: Mix all ingredients and cook pancakes on a griddle over medium heat. Serve with butter or sugar-free syrup.

**Lunch: Keto Shrimp and Avocado Salad**

**Ingredients:** 150g cooked shrimp, 1/2 avocado (diced), 2 cups mixed greens, 1 tbsp olive oil, 1 tbsp lime juice.

**Instructions:** Toss shrimp and avocado with mixed greens, olive oil, and lime juice.

**Dinner: Keto Pork Chops with Garlic Mushrooms**

**Ingredients:** 150g pork chops, 1 cup mushrooms (sliced), 2 tbsp butter, 1 garlic clove (minced), salt, and pepper.

**Instructions:** Cook pork chops in butter. Sauté mushrooms with garlic in the same pan until tender.

**Snacks:**

Cheese slices

A handful of pecans

## Day 40

**Breakfast: Keto Greek Yogurt Parfait**

**Ingredients:** Full-fat Greek yogurt (1/2 cup), nuts (1/4 cup), chia seeds (1 tbsp), blueberries (a few).

**Instructions:** Layer Greek yogurt with nuts, chia seeds, and blueberries.

**Lunch: Keto Beef Lettuce Wraps**

**Ingredients:** 150g ground beef, 1 tbsp soy sauce (low-carb), 1 tbsp olive oil, 1 cup shredded lettuce, 1/4 cup diced cucumber.

**Instructions:** Cook ground beef with soy sauce in olive oil. Serve in lettuce wraps with diced cucumber.

**Dinner: Keto Baked Chicken Thighs with Roasted Cauliflower**

**Ingredients:** 150g chicken thighs, 1 cup cauliflower florets, 2 tbsp olive oil, 1 tsp paprika, salt, and pepper.

**Instructions:** Preheat oven to 400°F (200°C). Rub chicken thighs with olive oil, paprika, salt, and pepper. Roast with cauliflower for 30 minutes.

**Snacks:**

Celery sticks with cream cheese

A handful of sunflower seeds

## Day 41

**Breakfast: Keto Egg and Cheese Breakfast Casserole**

**Ingredients:** Large eggs (4), shredded cheese (1/4 cup), heavy cream (1/4 cup), diced ham (1/2 cup), salt, pepper

**Instructions:** Preheat oven to 375°F (190°C). Mix all ingredients and pour into a greased baking dish. Bake for 25-30 minutes.

**Lunch: Keto Spinach and Feta Salad**

**Ingredients:** 2 cups spinach, 1/4 cup crumbled feta cheese, 1/4 cup sliced olives, 1 tbsp olive oil, 1 tbsp balsamic vinegar.

**Instructions:** Toss spinach with feta, olives, olive oil, and balsamic vinegar.

**Dinner: Keto Stuffed Portobello Mushrooms**

**Ingredients:** 2 large portobello mushrooms, 100g cream cheese, 1/4 cup shredded Parmesan cheese, 1 tbsp olive oil, salt, and pepper.

**Instructions:** Preheat oven to 375°F (190°C). Stuff mushrooms with cream cheese and Parmesan. Drizzle with olive oil and bake for 20 minutes.

**Snacks:**

A handful of mixed nuts

Keto-friendly chocolate bar

You should be well-acquainted with a variety of advanced meal options that not only support ketosis but also provide ample nutrition and satisfaction. This phase is crucial for solidifying your dietary habits and preparing for long-term success with Hyper Ketosis. Continue to monitor your macros, stay hydrated, and enjoy the diverse flavors and benefits of your ketogenic lifestyle.

## Adjusting Portions for Weight Loss and Maintenance

When following a Hyper Ketosis diet, adjusting your portions is essential to achieving your weight loss or maintenance goals. While the core principles of the diet remain the same, the specific portion sizes and calorie intake can vary depending on individual goals, activity levels, and metabolic needs. Here's a comprehensive guide to help you understand how to tailor your portions effectively.

### Understanding Caloric Needs

**Basal Metabolic Rate (BMR):**

BMR is the number of calories your body needs at rest to maintain basic physiological functions such as breathing, circulation, and cell production. You can estimate your BMR using formulas like the Harris-Benedict Equation or use online calculators.

## Men:

$BMR = 88.362 + (13.397 \times \text{weight in kg}) + (4.799 \times \text{height in cm}) - (5.677 \times \text{age in years})$

$BMR = 88.362 + (13.397 \times \text{weight in kg}) + (4.799 \times \text{height in cm}) - (5.677 \times \text{age in years})$

## Women:

$BMR = 447.593 + (9.247 \times \text{weight in kg}) + (3.098 \times \text{height in cm}) - (4.330 \times \text{age in years})$

$BMR = 447.593 + (9.247 \times \text{weight in kg}) + (3.098 \times \text{height in cm}) - (4.330 \times \text{age in years})$

Total Daily Energy Expenditure (TDEE):

TDEE, which considers your activity level, is calculated by multiplying your BMR by an activity factor:

For sedentary individuals (little or no exercise): Multiply your BMR by 1.2.

For lightly active individuals (light exercise/sports 1-3 days/week): Multiply your BMR by 1.375.

Moderately active (moderate exercise/sports 3-5 days/week): BMR × 1.55

For very active individuals (hard exercise/sports 6-7 days a week): Multiply your BMR by 1.725.

For super active individuals (very hard exercise/sports and a physical job): Multiply your BMR by 1.9.

Knowing your TDEE helps you determine how many calories you need to maintain your current weight.

### Adjusting Portions for Weight Loss

### Creating a Caloric Deficit:

To lose weight, you need to eat fewer calories than your TDEE. A typical approach is to reduce your calorie intake by 500 to 1,000 calories per day, which usually leads to a weight loss of about 1-2 pounds per week. However, for some people, a smaller deficit might be more manageable and still effective.

### Balancing Macronutrients:

**Fats:** On a ketogenic diet, fats should make up approximately 70-75% of your daily caloric intake. Focus on healthy fats such as avocados, nuts, seeds, and olive oil.

**Proteins:** Protein should constitute about 20-25% of your diet. Opt for high-quality protein: Choose lean meats, fish, eggs, and plant-based proteins as your protein sources.

**Carbohydrates:** Carbs should make up only 5-10% of your daily intake, mainly from non-starchy vegetables and low-carb fruits.

### Portion Control Techniques:

**Measure and Weigh Food:** Use a food scale and measuring cups to accurately portion your meals and snacks.

**Track Intake:** Utilize food tracking apps or journals to monitor your calorie and macronutrient intake.

**Focus on Satiety:** Prioritize foods that provide satiety, such as high-fiber vegetables and protein-rich foods, to help control hunger and avoid overeating.

### Adjusting Portions for Weight Maintenance

**Determining Maintenance Calories:**

Once you reach your desired weight, adjust your calorie intake to match your TDEE. This adjustment ensures that you maintain your weight without further loss or gain.

**Fine-Tuning Macronutrient Ratios:**

**Fats:** Maintain the same proportion as during weight loss but adjust the total fat intake to match your new caloric needs.

**Proteins:** Continue to consume adequate protein to support muscle mass and overall health.

**Carbohydrates:** You may slightly increase your carbohydrate intake while remaining in ketosis, but monitor how changes affect your ketosis levels.

**Implementing Sustainable Eating Habits:**

**Flexible Portions**: Allow for some flexibility in portion sizes while still adhering to your macro goals. This helps prevent feelings of deprivation and supports long-term adherence.

**Regular Monitoring:** Regularly check your weight and body measurements to ensure you remain within your target range.

**Adjust as Needed**: If you notice weight fluctuations, adjust your portion sizes and caloric intake accordingly.

**Individual Variation:**

Each person's metabolic rate and response to dietary changes can differ. It's important to listen to your body and adjust portions based on how you feel, energy levels, and progress towards your goals.

**Consulting Professionals:**

If you have specific health concerns or need personalized advice, consider consulting a registered dietitian or nutritionist who specializes in ketogenic diets. They can provide tailored recommendations based on your health profile and goals.

**Lifestyle Factors:**

Factors such as stress, sleep quality, and physical activity levels can impact your weight and portion needs. Pay attention to these aspects to support your overall success with the Hyper Ketosis diet.

# Chapter 4: The Best Foods for Hyper Ketosis

In the Hyper Ketosis diet, the quality and composition of your food play a critical role in maintaining and optimizing your state of ketosis. This chapter provides an extensive guide to the best foods that fit within this dietary framework, focusing on high-fat, low-carb options and proteins that support ketosis.

## High-Fat, Low-Carb Foods for Optimal Ketosis

Achieving and maintaining ketosis relies on consuming foods that are high in fat and low in carbohydrates. These foods not only support the metabolic state of ketosis but also provide essential nutrients to ensure overall health.

### Avocados:

**Nutritional Profile:** Avocados are rich in healthy monounsaturated fats, fiber, and various vitamins and minerals, including potassium, which helps maintain electrolyte balance.

**Benefits:** They provide a creamy texture to dishes and can be used in salads, smoothies, or as a spread. The high fat content makes avocados an excellent choice for sustaining ketosis and promoting satiety.

### Nuts and Seeds:

**Varieties:** Almonds, walnuts, chia seeds, flaxseeds, and hemp seeds.

**Nutritional Profile:** Nuts and seeds are high in healthy fats, protein, and fiber while being low in carbohydrates.

**Benefits:** They offer a convenient, nutrient-dense snack option and can be incorporated into various meals, including salads, yogurt, and baked goods. Chia and flaxseeds also provide omega-3 fatty acids, which are beneficial for heart health.

### Olive Oil:

**Nutritional Profile:** Extra virgin olive oil is high in monounsaturated fats and contains antioxidants like polyphenols.

**Benefits:** It is ideal for cooking, salad dressings, and drizzling over dishes. Olive oil helps increase the fat content of meals without adding significant carbs.

### Coconut Oil:

**Nutritional Profile:** Rich in medium-chain triglycerides (MCTs), which are rapidly absorbed and used for energy.

**Benefits:** Coconut oil supports ketosis by providing a quick source of ketones and can be used in cooking or baking. It is also stable at high temperatures, making it suitable for frying and sautéing.

### Butter and Ghee:

**Nutritional Profile:** Both are sources of saturated fats, which are stable for cooking. Ghee, a clarified butter, has additional benefits due to the removal of milk solids.

Benefits: They add rich flavor to dishes and can be used for cooking at high temperatures. Butter and ghee also contain fat-soluble vitamins A, D, E, and K.

**Cheese:**

**Varieties: Cheddar, mozzarella, cream cheese, and goat cheese.**

**Nutritional Profile:** Cheese is high in fat and protein, with minimal carbs.

**Benefits:** It provides a source of fat and protein while adding flavor and texture to meals. Cheese is a good source of calcium and other essential nutrients.

**Fatty Fish:**

**Varieties: Salmon, mackerel, sardines, and trout.**

**Nutritional Profile:** Fatty fish are packed with omega-3 fatty acids, high-quality protein, and low in carbs.

**Benefits:** These fish support heart health, brain function, and help maintain ketosis. They're perfect for meals that need a protein-packed, low-carb element.

**Low-Carb Vegetables:**

**Varieties:** Spinach, kale, broccoli, cauliflower, and zucchini.

**Nutritional Profile:** These vegetables are low in carbs and high in fiber, vitamins, and minerals.

**Benefits:** They provide essential nutrients and fiber while keeping carbohydrate intake low. They can be used in salads, side dishes, or as substitutes for higher-carb foods (e.g., cauliflower rice).

**Proteins That Support Ketosis**

Protein is an essential macronutrient that helps maintain muscle mass and supports metabolic functions. When following a Hyper Ketosis diet, it is crucial to choose proteins that complement the high-fat, low-carb nature of the diet.

**Lean Meats:**

**Varieties:** Chicken breast, turkey, lean cuts of beef and pork.

**Nutritional Profile**: High in protein and generally low in fat if choosing lean cuts.

**Benefits:** Provides a solid protein source while allowing you to control the fat content of your meals. Pairing lean meats with high-fat ingredients helps maintain ketosis.

**Fatty Meats:**

**Varieties:** Pork belly, ribeye steak, lamb chops.

**Nutritional Profile:** High in both fat and protein.

**Benefits:** These meats help meet fat requirements while offering a substantial protein source. They're great for maintaining ketosis and adding flavor to meals.

**Eggs:**

**Nutritional Profile:** Eggs are an excellent source of high-quality protein and healthy fats. A single large egg offers approximately 6 grams of protein and 5 grams of fat.

**Benefits:** Eggs are versatile and can be cooked in many different ways. They are also rich in essential nutrients such as choline and vitamins B12 and D. Including eggs in your diet can support muscle maintenance and overall health.

**Seafood:**

**Varieties:** Shrimp, crab, scallops, and shellfish.

**Nutritional Profile:** High in protein and typically low in carbs. Some seafood varieties, such as shrimp, are also low in fat.

**Benefits:** Seafood provides a high-quality protein source with minimal carbs. It also contains essential nutrients such as iodine and omega-3 fatty acids.

**Protein Powders:**

**Varieties:** Whey protein isolate, casein protein, collagen protein.

**Nutritional Profile:** High in protein with varying fat and carbohydrate content depending on the type.

**Benefits:** Protein powders can be a convenient way to supplement protein intake, especially when on the go. Choose powders with low or no added sugars and carbs.

**Tofu and Tempeh:**

**Nutritional Profile:** Both are soy-based products that offer plant-based protein. Tofu is lower in fat, while tempeh has a higher fat content.

**Benefits:** Suitable for vegetarians and vegans, tofu and tempeh can be included in a ketogenic diet when paired with high-fat ingredients.

**Greek Yogurt (Full-Fat):**

**Nutritional Profile:** Full-fat Greek yogurt is high in protein and fat while being relatively low in carbs compared to regular yogurt.

Benefits: It can be used as a base for snacks or meals and provides a good source of probiotics.

**Healthy Fats and Oils to Include**

Healthy fats are the cornerstone of the Hyper Ketosis diet, providing the primary energy source while helping to keep you in a state of ketosis. Choosing the right fats and oils is essential for maintaining health and achieving your dietary goals.

**Avocado Oil:**

**Nutritional Profile:** Avocado oil is high in monounsaturated fats and contains a moderate amount of omega-3 fatty acids.

**Benefits:** Avocado oil has a high smoke point (around 520°F/271°C), making it great for high-temperature cooking. It's also rich in antioxidants, which are beneficial for overall health.

**Coconut Oil:**

**Nutritional Profile:** Coconut oil is rich in medium-chain triglycerides (MCTs), which are quickly converted into ketones.

**Benefits:** MCTs offer a fast source of energy and support ketosis. Coconut oil is stable for cooking and has antimicrobial properties.

**Olive Oil:**

**Nutritional Profile:** Extra virgin olive oil is rich in monounsaturated fats and contains polyphenols with antioxidant properties.

**Benefits:** It is excellent for salad dressings, drizzling over dishes, or low-heat cooking. Olive oil supports heart health and offers essential nutrients.

### Butter and Ghee:

**Nutritional Profile:** Butter is high in saturated fats, while ghee (clarified butter) is also rich in healthy fats and free from milk solids.

**Benefits:** Both are suitable for cooking and baking. Ghee, in particular, has a higher smoke point and can be easier to digest for those with lactose intolerance.

### MCT Oil:

**Nutritional Profile:** MCT oil is composed of medium-chain fatty acids that are quickly absorbed and used for energy.

**Benefits:** It enhances ketone production and is commonly added to smoothies, coffee, or used as a supplement. MCT oil supports cognitive function and endurance.

### Flaxseed Oil:

**Nutritional Profile:** Flaxseed oil is rich in alpha-linolenic acid (ALA), a type of omega-3 fatty acid.

**Benefits:** It supports heart health and can be used in salad dressings or drizzled over foods. Avoid heating flaxseed oil: Flaxseed oil is sensitive to heat.

### Walnut Oil:

**Nutritional Profile:** Walnut oil is high in polyunsaturated fats and omega-3 fatty acids.

**Benefits:** It is best used in cold dishes, such as salads, due to its delicate flavor and lower smoke point. Walnut oil supports cardiovascular health and adds flavor to dishes.

## Ketosis-Friendly Vegetables

Vegetables are an essential part of a balanced ketogenic diet, providing fiber, vitamins, and minerals while keeping carbohydrate intake low. Selecting the right vegetables ensures you get the nutrients you need without disrupting ketosis.

### Leafy Greens:

**Varieties:** Spinach, kale, arugula, Swiss chard.

**Nutritional Profile:** Low in carbs and high in fiber, vitamins A, C, K, and various minerals.

**Benefits:** Leafy greens are nutrient-dense and versatile, perfect for salads, smoothies, or as a base for dishes.

### Cruciferous Vegetables:

**Varieties:** Broccoli, cauliflower, Brussels sprouts, cabbage.

**Nutritional Profile:** Low in carbs and high in fiber and antioxidants.

**Benefits:** Cruciferous vegetables support digestion and reduce inflammation. They can be used in stir-fries, roasted, or as substitutes for higher-carb foods (e.g., cauliflower rice).

### Zucchini:

**Nutritional Profile:** Low in carbs and calories, high in vitamins C and A, and antioxidants.

**Benefits:** Zucchini can be spiralized into noodles or used in baking. It provides a mild flavor and adds moisture to dishes.

### Bell Peppers:

**Varieties:** Red, green, yellow, and orange bell peppers.

**Nutritional Profile:** Moderate in carbs but high in vitamins A and C, and antioxidants.

**Benefits:** Bell peppers add color and crunch to dishes. They can be eaten raw, roasted, or added to salads and stir-fries.

### Asparagus:

**Nutritional Profile:** Low in carbs, high in fiber, and vitamins A, C, and K.

**Benefits:** Asparagus supports digestive health and can be grilled, steamed, or added to various dishes.

### Mushrooms:

**Varieties:** Button mushrooms, shiitake, portobello.

**Nutritional Profile:** Low in carbs and calories, high in vitamins B and D.

**Benefits:** Mushrooms add umami flavor and can be used in soups, stir-fries, or as a meat substitute.

### Avocado:

**Nutritional Profile:** High in monounsaturated fats and low in carbs.

**Benefits:** Avocados provide healthy fats, fiber, and essential nutrients. They can be added to salads, spread on toast, or enjoyed on their own.

### Keto Snacks and Beverages

Snacks and beverages play a significant role in keeping hunger at bay and maintaining energy levels while adhering to a Hyper Ketosis diet. Choosing keto-friendly options ensures you stay within your carbohydrate limits while enjoying satisfying treats.

### Keto Snacks:

**Nuts and Seeds:** Almonds, walnuts, macadamia nuts, chia seeds, and flaxseeds are packed with healthy fats and protein while being low in carbohydrates. Enjoy them on their own or mix them into yogurt or salads.

Cheese Crisps: Homemade or store-bought cheese crisps made from baked or fried cheese. They provide a crunchy, satisfying snack with minimal carbs.

**Olives:** Low-carb, high-fat. Olives make a great snack or can be added to salads and dishes for extra flavor.

**Jerky:** Look for sugar-free, low-carb jerky options. Beef, turkey, or chicken jerky can provide a protein-packed snack.

**Hard-Boiled Eggs:** A convenient, high-protein snack that fits well into a ketogenic diet. They can be seasoned and enjoyed on the go.

### Keto Beverages:

**Bulletproof Coffee:** Coffee concoction: Coffee blended with MCT oil and butter or ghee. It provides a fat boost and helps maintain ketosis while offering sustained energy.

**Herbal Teas:** Varieties like chamomile, peppermint, or rooibos are free from carbs and can be enjoyed hot or iced.

**Electrolyte Drinks:** Choose sugar-free electrolyte drinks to maintain hydration and electrolyte balance, especially during the adaptation phase.

**Unsweetened Almond Milk:** A low-carb alternative to dairy milk, suitable for smoothies or as a base for keto-friendly beverages.

**Sparkling Water:** Flavored or plain sparkling water provides hydration and can be a refreshing, zero-carb option.

**Ketosis-Friendly Smoothies:**

**Green Keto Smoothie:** Blend spinach, avocado, unsweetened almond milk, and a few berries for a low-carb, high-fat smoothie.

**Berry Keto Smoothie:** Use a small amount of low-carb berries like strawberries or raspberries, along with unsweetened almond milk and a scoop of protein powder for a refreshing drink.

# Chapter 5: Recipes for Hyper Ketosis Success

This chapter provides a selection of delicious and nutritious recipes tailored for the Hyper Ketosis diet. Each recipe is designed to help you stay in a state of ketosis while enjoying a variety of meals.

## Breakfast Recipes

### Avocado and Egg Breakfast Bowl

*Prep Time: 10 minutes*

*Cooking Time: 10 minutes*

*Nutritional Value: Calories: 350, Fat: 30g, Protein: 15g, Carbs: 10g*

**Ingredients:** 1 avocado, 2 eggs, 1 tbsp olive oil, salt, pepper, and optional toppings (e.g., sliced cherry tomatoes, fresh herbs).

**Instructions:**

1. Cut the avocado in half, remove the pit, and heat olive oil in a skillet over medium-high heat.

2. Cook the eggs to your preference (e.g., scrambled or fried).
3. Place the eggs inside the avocado halves.
4. Season with salt, pepper, and optional toppings.

### Keto Spinach and Feta Omelette

*Prep Time: 5 minutes*

*Cooking Time: 10 minutes*

*Nutritional Value: Calories: 320, Fat: 25g, Protein: 20g, Carbs: 7g*

**Ingredients:** 3 eggs, 1 cup fresh spinach, 1/4 cup crumbled feta cheese, 1 tbsp butter, salt, and pepper.

**Instructions:**

1. In a bowl, whisk together the eggs and add the salt and pepper.
2. In a pan over medium heat, melt the butter.
3. Add spinach and cook until wilted.

4. Pour eggs over spinach and cook until edges start to set.
5. Sprinkle feta cheese over one half and fold the omelette.

### Chia Seed Pudding with Berries

*Prep Time: 5 minutes*

*Cooking Time: 0 minutes (refrigeration time: 4 hours)*

*Nutritional Value: Calories: 250, Fat: 15g, Protein: 8g, Carbs: 20g (net carbs: 10g)*

**Ingredients:** 1/4 cup chia seeds, 1 cup unsweetened almond milk, 1 tbsp chia seeds, 1/2 cup mixed berries.

**Instructions:**

1. Combine chia seeds and almond milk in a bowl or jar.
2. After giving it a good stir, wait five minutes before stirring again. For at least four hours or overnight, cover and chill.
3. Top with berries before serving.

### Keto Breakfast Smoothie

*Prep Time: 5 minutes*

*Cooking Time: 0 minutes*

*Nutritional Value: Calories: 300, Fat: 25g, Protein: 15g, Carbs: 8g (net carbs: 5g)*

**Ingredients:** 1 cup unsweetened almond milk, 1/2 avocado, 1 scoop protein powder, 1 tbsp MCT oil, 1/4 cup spinach.

**Instructions:**

1. Blend all ingredients until smooth.
2. Serve immediately.

### Bacon and Egg Muffins

*Prep Time: 10 minutes*

*Cooking Time: 20 minutes*

*Nutritional Value: Calories: 250, Fat: 20g, Protein: 15g, Carbs: 2g*

**Ingredients:** 6 eggs, 6 strips bacon, 1/4 cup shredded cheddar cheese, salt, and pepper.

**Instructions:**

1. Preheat oven to 375°F (190°C).
2. Cook bacon in a skillet until crispy and crumble.
3. Whisk eggs with salt and pepper.
4. Line a muffin tin with bacon strips.
5. After adding cheese on top, pour the eggs into the muffin cups.
6. Bake for 20 minutes or until set.

### Greek Yogurt with Nuts and Seeds

*Prep Time: 5 minutes*

*Cooking Time: 0 minutes*

*Nutritional Value: Calories: 280, Fat: 20g, Protein: 15g, Carbs: 12g (net carbs: 7g)*

**Ingredients:** 1 cup full-fat Greek yogurt, 1 tbsp chia seeds, 1 tbsp flaxseeds, 10 almonds.

**Instructions:**

1. Mix yogurt with chia seeds and flaxseeds.
2. Top with almonds before serving.

### Egg and Avocado Breakfast Wrap

*Prep Time: 10 minutes*

*Cooking Time: 10 minutes*

*Nutritional Value: Calories: 300, Fat: 22g, Protein: 15g, Carbs: 8g (net carbs: 4g)*

**Ingredients:** 2 eggs, 1/2 avocado, 1 low-carb tortilla, 1 tbsp olive oil.

**Instructions:**

1. Heat olive oil in a skillet and scramble the eggs.
2. Slice avocado and place on the tortilla.
3. Add scrambled eggs on top of avocado.
4. After rolling the tortilla, cut it in half.

### Keto Pancakes

*Prep Time: 10 minutes*

*Cooking Time: 10 minutes*

*Nutritional Value: Calories: 350, Fat: 30g, Protein: 15g, Carbs: 8g (net carbs: 5g)*

**Ingredients:** 1 cup almond flour, 2 eggs, 1/4 cup unsweetened almond milk, 1 tbsp coconut oil, 1 tsp baking powder.

**Instructions:**

1. Mix all ingredients in a bowl.
2. In a pan over medium heat, preheat the coconut oil.
3. To make pancakes, pour batter onto the skillet.
4. Cook until bubbles appear, then turn and continue cooking until the food becomes golden brown.

### Stuffed Bell Peppers with Egg

*Prep Time: 10 minutes*

*Cooking Time: 20 minutes*

*Nutritional Value: Calories: 250, Fat: 18g, Protein: 12g, Carbs: 10g (net carbs: 6g)*

**Ingredients:** 2 bell peppers, 2 eggs, 1/4 cup shredded cheese, salt, and pepper.

**Instructions:**

1.  Preheat oven to 375°F (190°C).
2.  Remove the seeds from the bell peppers by cutting off the tops.
3.  Place bell peppers in a baking dish.
4.  Crack an egg into each bell pepper and top with cheese.
5.  Bake for 20 minutes or until eggs are set.

### Salmon and Cream Cheese Breakfast Bites

*Prep Time: 10 minutes*

*Cooking Time: 0 minutes*

*Nutritional Value: Calories: 280, Fat: 20g, Protein: 15g, Carbs: 2g*

**Ingredients:** 4 oz smoked salmon, 2 oz cream cheese, 1 tbsp capers, fresh dill.

**Instructions:**

1.  Spread cream cheese on salmon slices.
2.  Top with capers and fresh dill.
3.  Roll up and slice into bite-sized pieces.

## Lunch Recipes

### Grilled Chicken Salad with Avocado Dressing

*Prep Time: 15 minutes*

*Cooking Time: 10 minutes*

*Nutritional Value: Calories: 350, Fat: 28g, Protein: 25g, Carbs: 8g (net carbs: 5g)*

**Ingredients:** 1 chicken breast, 2 cups mixed greens, 1 avocado, 2 tbsp olive oil, 1 tbsp lemon juice, salt, and pepper.

**Instructions:**

1. Grill chicken breasts until thoroughly done, then slice.
2. Combine mixed greens with sliced chicken.
3. Blend avocado, olive oil, lemon juice, salt, and pepper to make dressing.
4. Toss salad with avocado dressing.

### Zucchini Noodles with Pesto

*Prep Time: 10 minutes*

*Cooking Time: 10 minutes*

*Nutritional Value: Calories: 280, Fat: 22g, Protein: 8g, Carbs: 10g (net carbs: 5g)*

**Ingredients:** 2 zucchinis, 1/4 cup pesto, 1 tbsp olive oil, grated Parmesan cheese.

**Instructions:**

1. Spiralize zucchinis into noodles.
2. Heat olive oil in a skillet and sauté zucchini noodles for 5 minutes.
3. Add some pesto and sprinkle some Parmesan cheese on top.

### Beef and Broccoli Stir-Fry

*Prep Time: 15 minutes*

*Cooking Time: 10 minutes*

*Nutritional Value: Calories: 300, Fat: 22g, Protein: 25g, Carbs: 12g (net carbs: 7g)*

**Ingredients:** 8 oz beef strips, 2 cups broccoli florets, 2 tbsp soy sauce, 1 tbsp sesame oil, 1 clove garlic, minced.

**Instructions:**

1. Heat sesame oil in a skillet and cook garlic until fragrant.
2. Add beef strips and cook until browned.
3. Add broccoli and soy sauce and stir-fry until tender-crisp.

## Stuffed Bell Peppers with Ground Turkey

*Prep Time: 15 minutes*

*Cooking Time: 25 minutes*

*Nutritional Value: Calories: 300, Fat: 18g, Protein: 25g, Carbs: 12g (net carbs: 8g)*

**Ingredients:** 4 bell peppers, 1 lb ground turkey, 1 cup cauliflower rice, 1/2 cup shredded cheese, 1 tsp Italian seasoning.

**Instructions:**

1. Preheat oven to 375°F (190°C).
2. Cook ground turkey with Italian seasoning until browned.
3. Mix with cauliflower rice and stuff into bell peppers.
4. Add cheese on top, then bake for twenty-five minutes.

## Salmon Avocado Salad and

*Prep Time: 10 minutes*

*Cooking Time: 10 minutes (if using cooked salmon)*

*Nutritional Value: Calories: 350, Fat: 25g, Protein: 25g, Carbs: 8g (net carbs: 5g)*

**Ingredients:** 1 can salmon, 1 avocado, 2 cups mixed greens, 1 tbsp olive oil, 1 tbsp lemon juice, salt, and pepper.

**Instructions:**

1. Flake salmon and combine with avocado chunks and mixed greens.
2. Drizzle with olive oil and lemon juice.
3. Season with salt and pepper before serving.

## Keto Chicken Caesar Salad

*Prep Time: 10 minutes*

*Cooking Time: 15 minutes (for chicken)*

*Nutritional Value: Calories: 320, Fat: 25g, Protein: 25g, Carbs: 6g (net carbs: 4g)*

**Ingredients:** 1 chicken breast, 2 cups romaine lettuce, 1/4 cup Caesar dressing (keto-friendly), 1/4 cup Parmesan cheese.

**Instructions:**

1. Grill or cook chicken breast and slice.
2. Toss lettuce with Caesar dressing.
3. Top with chicken and Parmesan cheese.

## Creamy Avocado Chicken Soup

*Prep Time: 10 minutes*

*Cooking Time: 20 minutes*

*Nutritional Value: Calories: 320, Fat: 22g, Protein: 25g, Carbs: 10g (net carbs: 6g)*

**Ingredients:** 2 cups chicken broth, 1 avocado, 1 cup cooked chicken, 1/4 cup heavy cream, 1 clove garlic, minced.

**Instructions:**

1. Blend avocado with chicken broth until smooth.
2. Heat in a saucepan and add cooked chicken.
3. Stir in heavy cream and garlic, and heat through.

## Egg Salad Lettuce Wraps

*Prep Time: 10 minutes*

*Cooking Time: 10 minutes (for boiling eggs)*

*Nutritional Value: Calories: 250, Fat: 20g, Protein: 15g, Carbs: 5g (net carbs: 3g)*

**Ingredients:** 4 hard-boiled eggs, 1/4 cup mayo, 1 tbsp Dijon mustard, lettuce leaves, salt, and pepper.

**Instructions:**

1. Chop hard-boiled eggs and combine with mayo and Dijon mustard.
2. Season with salt and pepper.
3. Serve in lettuce leaves as wraps.

### Spaghetti Squash with Alfredo Sauce

*Prep Time: 15 minutes*

*Cooking Time: 40 minutes*

*Nutritional Value: Calories: 300, Fat: 22g, Protein: 12g, Carbs: 15g (net carbs: 10g)*

**Ingredients:** 1 spaghetti squash, 1 cup heavy cream, 1/2 cup grated Parmesan cheese, 2 tbsp butter, salt, and pepper.

**Instructions:**

1. Roast spaghetti squash at 400°F (200°C) for 40 minutes.
2. Scrape out strands with a fork.
3. Heat butter in a saucepan, add heavy cream and Parmesan cheese to make Alfredo sauce.
4. Toss squash with sauce.

### Keto Tuna Salad

*Prep Time: 10 minutes*

*Cooking Time: 0 minutes*

*Nutritional Value: Calories: 250, Fat: 20g, Protein: 20g, Carbs: 5g (net carbs: 2g)*

**Ingredients:** 1 can tuna, 2 tbsp mayo, 1 celery stalk, chopped, 1 tbsp lemon juice, salt, and pepper.

**Instructions:**

1. Mix tuna with mayo, celery, and lemon juice.
2. Season with salt and pepper.
3. Serve chilled.

## Dinner Recipes

### Baked Salmon with Lemon and Dill

*Prep Time: 10 minutes*

*Cooking Time: 20 minutes*

*Nutritional Value: Calories: 350, Fat: 25g, Protein: 30g, Carbs: 5g (net carbs: 2g)*

**Ingredients:** 4 oz salmon fillet, 1 lemon (sliced), 1 tbsp fresh dill, 1 tbsp olive oil, salt, and pepper.

**Instructions:**

1. Preheat oven to 375°F (190°C).
2. Place salmon fillet on a baking sheet.
3. Drizzle with olive oil and top with lemon slices and dill.
4. Bake until the salmon is cooked through and flakes easily with a fork or for twenty minutes

## Zucchini Lasagna

*Prep Time: 15 minutes*

*Cooking Time: 30 minutes*

*Nutritional Value: Calories: 300, Fat: 20g, Protein: 15g, Carbs: 12g (net carbs: 8g)*

**Ingredients:** 3 large zucchinis (sliced thin), 1 cup ricotta cheese, 1 cup marinara sauce (keto-friendly), 1/2 cup shredded mozzarella, 1/2 lb ground beef, 1/2 tsp Italian seasoning.

**Instructions:**

1. Preheat oven to 375°F (190°C).
2. Cook ground beef with Italian seasoning until browned.
3. Layer zucchini slices, ricotta, beef, and marinara sauce in a baking dish.
4. Top with mozzarella cheese and bake for 30 minutes.

## Creamy Garlic Chicken

*Prep Time: 10 minutes*

*Cooking Time: 20 minutes*

*Nutritional Value: Calories: 350, Fat: 25g, Protein: 30g, Carbs: 6g (net carbs: 4g)*

**Ingredients:** 2 chicken breasts, 1/2 cup heavy cream, 1/4 cup grated Parmesan cheese, 2 cloves garlic (minced), 2 tbsp olive oil.

**Instructions:**

1. In a pan over medium heat, warm the olive oil.
2. Chicken breasts should be cooked thoroughly and golden brown.
3. When aromatic, add the garlic and simmer.

4. Cook until the sauce thickens, stirring in the heavy cream and Parmesan cheese.

## Stuffed Portobello Mushrooms

*Prep Time: 10 minutes*

*Cooking Time: 20 minutes*

*Nutritional Value: Calories: 280, Fat: 22g, Protein: 10g, Carbs: 12g (net carbs: 6g)*

**Ingredients:** 4 large portobello mushrooms, 1/2 cup cream cheese, 1/4 cup grated Parmesan cheese, 1/4 cup chopped spinach, 1 tbsp olive oil.

**Instructions:**

1. Preheat oven to 375°F (190°C).
2. Mix cream cheese, Parmesan, spinach, and olive oil.
3. Stuff mushrooms with the mixture and place on a baking sheet.
4. Bake the mushrooms for twenty minutes at a time or until they are soft.

## Beef and Cauliflower Rice Stir-Fry

*Prep Time: 10 minutes*

*Cooking Time: 15 minutes*

*Nutritional Value: Calories: 300, Fat: 20g, Protein: 25g, Carbs: 10g (net carbs: 6g)*

**Ingredients:** 8 oz beef strips, 2 cups cauliflower rice, 2 tbsp soy sauce, 1 tbsp sesame oil, 1 bell pepper (sliced).

**Instructions:**

1. Heat sesame oil in a skillet and cook beef strips until browned.
2. Add bell pepper and cook until tender.
3. Stir in cauliflower rice and soy sauce, cooking until rice is tender.

### Chicken and Broccoli Alfredo

*Prep Time: 10 minutes*

*Cooking Time: 20 minutes*

*Nutritional Value: Calories: 320, Fat: 22g, Protein: 25g, Carbs: 10g (net carbs: 6g)*

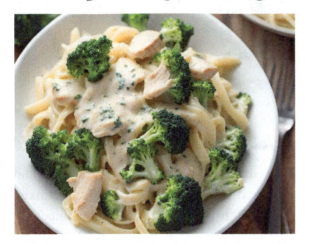

**Ingredients:** 2 chicken breasts, 2 cups broccoli florets, 1 cup heavy cream, 1/2 cup Parmesan cheese, 1 tbsp olive oil.

**Instructions:**

1. Cook chicken breasts in olive oil until fully cooked.
2. Add broccoli and cook until tender.
3. Cook until the sauce thickens, stirring in the heavy cream and Parmesan cheese.

### Pork Chops with Creamy Mushroom Sauce

*Prep Time: 10 minutes*

*Cooking Time: 25 minutes*

*Nutritional Value: Calories: 340, Fat: 25g, Protein: 30g, Carbs: 8g (net carbs: 5g)*

**Ingredients:** 2 pork chops, 1 cup mushrooms (sliced), 1/2 cup heavy cream, 2 tbsp olive oil, 1 tbsp Dijon mustard.

**Instructions:**

1. Heat olive oil in a skillet and cook pork chops until browned.
2. Remove pork and set aside.
3. Add mushrooms to the skillet and cook until soft.
4. Stir in heavy cream and Dijon mustard, cooking until sauce thickens.
5. Return pork chops to the skillet and coat with sauce.

### Keto Meatballs with Marinara

*Prep Time: 15 minutes*

*Cooking Time: 30 minutes*

*Nutritional Value: Calories: 350, Fat: 25g, Protein: 20g, Carbs: 8g (net carbs: 5g)*

**Ingredients:** 1 lb ground beef, 1/2 cup almond flour, 1/4 cup grated Parmesan cheese, 1 egg, 1 cup marinara sauce (keto-friendly).

**Instructions:**

1. Preheat oven to 375°F (190°C).
2. Mix ground beef, almond flour, Parmesan cheese, and egg.
3. Form into meatballs and place on a baking sheet.
4. Bake for 20 minutes, then top with marinara sauce and bake for an additional 10 minutes.

### Thai Chicken Curry

*Prep Time: 10 minutes*

*Cooking Time: 25 minutes*

*Nutritional Value: Calories: 350, Fat: 28g, Protein: 20g, Carbs: 12g (net carbs: 8g)*

**Ingredients:** 2 chicken breasts, 1 can coconut milk, 2 tbsp Thai red curry paste, 1 cup bell peppers (sliced), 1 tbsp fish sauce.

**Instructions:**

1. Heat curry paste in a skillet and add chicken, cooking until browned.
2. Stir in coconut milk and fish sauce, bringing to a simmer.
3. Add bell peppers and cook until tender.

### Shrimp and Avocado Salad

*Prep Time: 15 minutes*

*Cooking Time: 10 minutes*

*Nutritional Value: Calories: 300, Fat: 22g, Protein: 20g, Carbs: 10g (net carbs: 6g)*

**Ingredients:** 1 lb shrimp (peeled and deveined), 1 avocado (diced), 2 cups mixed greens, 2 tbsp olive oil, 1 tbsp lime juice.

**Instructions:**

1. Cook shrimp in olive oil until pink and cooked through.
2. Combine with avocado and mixed greens.
3. Drizzle with olive oil and lime juice.

## Snack Recipes

### Cheese and Pepperoni Crisps

*Prep Time: 5 minutes*

*Cooking Time: 10 minutes*

*Nutritional Value: Calories: 200, Fat: 16g, Protein: 12g, Carbs: 2g*

**Ingredients:** 1/2 cup shredded cheddar cheese, 10 slices pepperoni.

**Instructions:**

1. Preheat oven to 375°F (190°C).
2. Place cheese in small mounds on a baking sheet.
3. Top with pepperoni slices.
4. Bake for 10 minutes or until cheese is crispy.

### Guacamole with Veggie Sticks

*Prep Time: 10 minutes*

*Cooking Time: 0 minutes*

*Nutritional Value: Calories: 250, Fat: 20g, Protein: 3g, Carbs: 15g (net carbs: 8g)*

**Ingredients:** 2 avocados, 1/2 onion (chopped), 1 tomato (diced), 1 lime (juiced), 1 cup celery and cucumber sticks.

**Instructions:**

1. Mash avocados and combine with lime juice, tomato, and onion.
2. Serve with celery and cucumber sticks.

### Almond Butter Celery Sticks

*Prep Time: 5 minutes*

*Cooking Time: 0 minutes*

*Nutritional Value: Calories: 150, Fat: 12g, Protein: 4g, Carbs: 8g (net carbs: 5g)*

**Ingredients:** 4 celery sticks, 2 tbsp almond butter.

**Instructions:**

1. Spread almond butter onto celery sticks.
2. Enjoy immediately.

## Keto Energy Balls

*Prep Time: 10 minutes*

*Cooking Time: 0 minutes (chill time: 30 minutes)*

*Nutritional Value: Calories: 200, Fat: 18g, Protein: 5g, Carbs: 5g (net carbs: 2g)*

**Ingredients:** 1 cup almond flour, 1/2 cup unsweetened shredded coconut, 1/4 cup almond butter, 1/4 cup chia seeds, 1 tbsp erythritol.

**Instructions:**

1. Mix all ingredients in a bowl.
2. Roll into bite-sized balls.
3. Chill in the refrigerator for 30 minutes.

## Spicy Roasted Nuts

*Prep Time: 5 minutes*

*Cooking Time: 15 minutes*

*Nutritional Value: Calories: 200, Fat: 18g, Protein: 6g, Carbs: 6g (net carbs: 3g)*

**Ingredients:** 1 cup mixed nuts, 1 tbsp olive oil, 1 tsp paprika, 1/2 tsp cayenne pepper, salt.

**Instructions:**

1. Preheat oven to 350°F (175°C).
2. Toss nuts with olive oil and spices.
3. Place evenly onto a baking sheet and bake for fifteen minutes.

## Greek Yogurt with Berries

*Prep Time: 5 minutes*

*Cooking Time: 0 minutes*

*Nutritional Value: Calories: 150, Fat: 8g, Protein: 10g, Carbs: 10g (net carbs: 6g)*

**Ingredients:** 1/2 cup Greek yogurt, 1/4 cup mixed berries, 1 tsp chia seeds.

**Instructions:**

1. Mix Greek yogurt with berries and chia seeds.
2. Serve chilled.

## Hard-Boiled Eggs

*Prep Time: 5 minutes*

*Cooking Time: 10 minutes*

*Nutritional Value: Calories: 70 per egg, Fat: 5g, Protein: 6g, Carbs: 1g*

**Ingredients:** Eggs.

**Instructions:**

1. Put the eggs in a saucepan and pour water over them.
2. After bringing to a boil, lower heat, and simmer for ten minutes.
3. Cool in ice water and peel.

## Avocado and Tuna Salad

*Prep Time: 10 minutes*

*Cooking Time: 0 minutes*

*Nutritional Value: Calories: 250, Fat: 20g, Protein: 15g, Carbs: 8g (net carbs: 5g)*

**Ingredients:** 1 avocado, 1 can tuna, 1 tbsp olive oil, 1 tbsp lemon juice, salt, and pepper.

**Instructions:**

1. Add lemon juice, olive oil, and avocado to tuna.
2. Season with salt and pepper.

## Cucumber and Hummus

*Prep Time: 5 minutes*

*Cooking Time: 0 minutes*

*Nutritional Value: Calories: 150, Fat: 10g, Protein: 5g, Carbs: 10g (net carbs: 6g)*

**Ingredients:** 1 cucumber (sliced), 1/4 cup hummus (keto-friendly).

**Instructions:**

1. Serve cucumber slices with hummus for dipping.

## Keto Chocolate Avocado Pudding

*Prep Time: 10 minutes*

*Cooking Time: 0 minutes (chill time: 30 minutes)*

*Nutritional Value: Calories: 250, Fat: 20g, Protein: 4g, Carbs: 15g (net carbs: 7g)*

**Ingredients:** 1 avocado, 2 tbsp cocoa powder, 2 tbsp erythritol, 1/4 cup almond milk, 1 tsp vanilla extract.

**Instructions:**

2. Blend all ingredients until smooth.
3. Chill in the refrigerator for 30 minutes before serving.

# Desserts

### Keto Chocolate Avocado Mousse

*Prep Time: 10 minutes*

*Cooking Time: 0 minutes (Chill Time: 30 minutes)*

*Nutritional Value: Calories: 250, Fat: 22g, Protein: 4g, Carbs: 15g (Net Carbs: 7g)*

**Ingredients:** 1/4 cup unsweetened cocoa powder, 2 tablespoons erythritol, 1/4 cup almond milk, 1 tsp vanilla extract, and 2 ripe avocados.

**Instructions:**

1. Scoop avocado flesh into a blender.
2. Add cocoa powder, erythritol, almond milk, and vanilla extract.
3. Blend until smooth and creamy.
4. Chill in the refrigerator for at least 30 minutes before serving.

### Almond Flour Brownies

**Prep Time: 15 minutes**

**Cooking Time: 25 minutes**

**Nutritional Value: Calories: 180 per serving (1 brownie), Fat: 15g, Protein: 5g, Carbs: 10g (Net Carbs: 4g)**

**Ingredients:** 1 cup almond flour, 1/2 cup unsweetened cocoa powder, 1/4 cup erythritol, 1/4 cup melted butter, 2 eggs, 1 tsp vanilla extract.

**Instructions:**

1. Preheat the oven to 350°F (175°C), and place parchment paper inside an 8-by-8-inch baking pan.
2. In a bowl, combine erythritol, cocoa powder, and almond flour.
3. Add melted butter, eggs, and vanilla extract. Mix until smooth.
4. Pour batter into the pan and bake for 25 minutes.

### Keto Cheesecake Bites

*Prep Time: 15 minutes*

*Cooking Time: 15 minutes (Chill Time: 1 hour)*

*Nutritional Value: Calories: 180, Fat: 16g, Protein: 6g, Carbs: 6g (Net Carbs: 4g)*

**Ingredients:** 1 cup cream cheese, 1/4 cup erythritol, 1 tsp vanilla extract, 1/2 cup crushed nuts (for crust).

**Instructions:**

1. Beat cream cheese, erythritol, and vanilla extract until smooth.
2. Spoon mixture into silicone molds.
3. Top with crushed nuts.
4. Before serving, let it freeze for at least an hour.

## Coconut Macaroons

*Prep Time: 10 minutes*

*Cooking Time: 15 minutes*

*Nutritional Value: Calories: 120 per macaroon, Fat: 10g, Protein: 2g, Carbs: 8g (Net Carbs: 5g)*

**Ingredients:** 2 cups unsweetened shredded coconut, 1/4 cup almond flour, 1/4 cup erythritol, 2 egg whites.

**Instructions:**

1. Adjust the oven temperature to 350°F (175°C) and place parchment paper on a baking pan.
2. Mix all ingredients in a bowl.
3. Spoon mixture onto the baking sheet in small amounts.
4. Bake for 15 minutes until golden brown.

## Frozen Berry Yogurt Bars

*Prep Time: 10 minutes*

*Cooking Time: 0 minutes (Freeze Time: 2 hours)*

*Nutritional Value: Calories: 120 per bar, Fat: 6g, Protein: 5g, Carbs: 12g (Net Carbs: 6g)*

**Ingredients:** 1 cup Greek yogurt, 1/2 cup mixed berries, 1 tbsp erythritol, 1 tsp vanilla extract.

**Instructions:**

1. Mix Greek yogurt, erythritol, and vanilla extract in a bowl.
2. Fold in mixed berries.
3. Pour mixture into a lined baking dish and freeze for 2 hours.
4. Cut into bars and serve.

## Pumpkin Spice Chia Pudding

*Prep Time: 5 minutes*

*Cooking Time: 0 minutes (Chill Time: 4 hours)*

*Nutritional Value: Calories: 180, Fat: 12g, Protein: 5g, Carbs: 15g (Net Carbs: 7g)*

**Ingredients:** 1/4 cup chia seeds, 1 cup unsweetened almond milk, 1/4 cup pumpkin puree, 1/2 tsp pumpkin pie spice, 1 tbsp erythritol.

**Instructions:**

1. Combine chia seeds, almond milk, pumpkin puree, pumpkin pie spice, and erythritol in a bowl.
2. After thoroughly stirring, chill for four hours or overnight.
3. Serve chilled.

## Ricotta and Berry Parfait

*Prep Time: 10 minutes*

*Cooking Time: 0 minutes*

*Nutritional Value: Calories: 250, Fat: 15g, Protein: 12g, Carbs: 15g (Net Carbs: 8g)*

**Ingredients:** 1 cup ricotta cheese, 1/2 cup mixed berries, 1 tbsp chia seeds, 1 tbsp honey (optional).

**Instructions:**

1. Layer ricotta cheese, mixed berries, and chia seeds in serving glasses.
2. Drizzle with honey if desired.
3. Serve right away or let cool for a little while.

## Keto Peanut Butter Cookies

*Prep Time: 10 minutes*

*Cooking Time: 12 minutes*

*Nutritional Value: Calories: 150 per cookie, Fat: 12g, Protein: 5g, Carbs: 8g (Net Carbs: 4g)*

**Ingredients:** 1 cup peanut butter, 1/2 cup erythritol, 1 egg, 1/2 tsp vanilla extract.

**Instructions:**

1. Adjust the oven temperature to 350°F (175°C) and place parchment paper on a baking pan.
2. Mix all ingredients until well combined.

3. Drop spoonful of dough onto the baking sheet and flatten slightly.
4. Bake for 12 minutes until edges are golden.

## Chocolate-Covered Strawberries

*Prep Time: 10 minutes*

*Cooking Time: 5 minutes (Chill Time: 30 minutes)*

*Nutritional Value: Calories: 120 per strawberry, Fat: 10g, Protein: 2g, Carbs: 10g (Net Carbs: 5g)*

**Ingredients:** 1 cup dark chocolate (85% or higher), 10 fresh strawberries.

**Instructions:**

1. Use a double boiler or the microwave to melt dark chocolate.
2. Dip strawberries in melted chocolate and place on a parchment-lined tray.
3. To set, refrigerate for thirty minutes.

# Chapter 6: Overcoming Plateaus and Challenges

Maintaining a Hyper Ketosis diet can be a powerful tool for achieving optimal health and weight loss. However, like any dietary regimen, it comes with its challenges. Understanding why plateaus occur and how to effectively overcome them can make the difference between a temporary stall and sustained success. This chapter delves into common reasons for stalling in ketosis and provides actionable strategies for breaking through weight loss plateaus.

## Common Reasons for Stalling in Ketosis

Experiencing a stall in your ketogenic journey can be frustrating, but it's important to recognize that it's a common part of the process. Understanding the potential causes can help you address and overcome these obstacles.

### Inaccurate Tracking

**Description:** One of the most common reasons for a stall is inaccurate tracking of macronutrients. Many people underestimate or overestimate their fat, protein, and carbohydrate intake.

**Solution:** Use a food diary or a tracking app to log everything you eat. Ensure you are measuring portion sizes accurately and consistently reviewing your macros to stay within your target ranges.

### Hidden Carbs

**Description:** Carbohydrates can sneak into your diet through sauces, dressings, or processed foods that may not be obvious.

**Solution:** Read food labels carefully and choose whole, unprocessed foods. Opt for homemade dressings and sauces where you can control the ingredients.

### Inadequate Fat Intake

**Description:** A ketogenic diet requires a high-fat intake to maintain ketosis. If you're not consuming enough fat, your body may not stay in ketosis.

**Solution:** Increase your intake of healthy fats such as avocados, olive oil, and nuts. Ensure that fats make up a significant portion of your daily calorie intake.

### Overconsumption of Protein

**Description:** Excessive protein intake can lead to gluconeogenesis, where protein is converted into glucose, potentially disrupting ketosis.

**Solution:** Keep an eye on your protein consumption to make sure it meets your specific demands. Typically, protein should be moderate, with fat being the primary energy source.

### Stress and Lack of Sleep

**Description:** High stress levels and inadequate sleep can impact your metabolic rate and hormone balance, affecting ketosis.

Solution: Incorporate stress-reducing activities such as meditation, yoga, or deep breathing exercises. Aim for seven to nine hours of good sleep every night.

### Medical Conditions and Medications

**Description:** Certain medical conditions and medications can affect ketosis and weight loss.

Solution: Consult with a healthcare provider to ensure that any medical conditions or medications are not interfering with your diet. They can provide guidance or adjustments if needed.

### Dehydration and Electrolyte Imbalance

**Description:** Increased water loss and electrolyte imbalance are two possible effects of ketosis.

**Solution:** Stay hydrated by drinking plenty of water. Ensure adequate intake of electrolytes such as sodium, potassium, and magnesium through diet or supplements.

### Adapting to New Exercise Routines

**Description:** Starting or changing your exercise routine can temporarily affect weight loss as your body adjusts.

Solution: Monitor your exercise intensity and frequency. Allow time for your body to adapt and maintain consistency in your workouts.

## How to Get Past a Plateau in Your Weight Loss

Breaking through a weight loss plateau involves reassessing and adjusting various aspects of your diet and lifestyle. Here are some strategies to help you overcome these stalls and continue progressing toward your goals.

### Reevaluate Your Macronutrient Ratios

**Description:** A plateau may indicate that your current macronutrient ratios are no longer optimal.

**Solution:** Recalculate your macronutrient needs and adjust your fat, protein, and carbohydrate intake as needed. You might need to increase fat intake or reduce protein slightly to rebalance.

### Increase Physical Activity

**Description:** Your body may become accustomed to your current exercise routine, leading to a plateau.

**Solution:** Introduce new forms of exercise or increase the intensity of your workouts. To increase metabolism and encourage fat reduction, combine strength and aerobic exercise.

### Implement Intermittent Fasting

**Description:** Intermittent fasting can help improve metabolic flexibility and enhance ketosis.

**Solution:** Try incorporating intermittent fasting protocols such as 16/8 (16 hours of fasting, 8-hour eating window) to boost fat burning and overcome plateaus.

### Adjust Portion Sizes

**Description:** Even within a ketogenic framework, portion sizes can impact weight loss.

**Solution:** Review and adjust your portion sizes to ensure you're not consuming more calories than you need. Smaller, balanced meals may help with continued progress.

### Cycle Your Carbs

**Description:** Occasionally increasing carbohydrate intake can help reset metabolic processes and break through a plateau.

**Solution:** Implement a targeted carb cycling approach where you have specific days with slightly higher carb intake, ensuring these carbs come from keto-friendly sources.

### Monitor and Reduce Hidden Sources of Calories

**Description:** Hidden calories from snacks, drinks, or condiments can add up.

**Solution:** Be vigilant about all sources of calories and ensure they are accounted for. Opt for whole foods and minimize or eliminate hidden calorie sources.

### Track and Analyze Your Progress

**Description:** Tracking your progress and analyzing patterns can help identify what may be causing the plateau.

**Solution:** Use tracking tools to review your dietary intake, physical activity, and other lifestyle factors. Look for trends or changes that might have led to the stall.

### Consult with a Professional

**Description:** Sometimes, professional guidance is necessary to address complex issues.

**Solution:** Work with a nutritionist or dietitian specializing in ketogenic diets. They can provide personalized advice and adjustments based on your individual needs and goals.

### Adjusting Your Diet for Continued Progress

To ensure sustained progress on a Hyper Ketosis diet, regular adjustments and fine-tuning may be necessary. Here's how you can optimize your diet for continued success:

### Recalibrate Your Macronutrient Ratios

**Understanding Macronutrient Balance:** The balance between fats, proteins, and carbohydrates is crucial for maintaining ketosis. As your body adapts, you may need to adjust these ratios.

**How to Adjust:**

**Increase Fat Intake:** If you're experiencing a stall, consider increasing your fat intake slightly. This helps ensure that fat remains your primary energy source.

**Moderate Protein:** Ensure protein intake is moderate and not excessive, as too much protein can be converted into glucose.

**Lower Carbs:** Review your carbohydrate intake and make sure you're staying within your target range for ketosis.

**Track and Analyze Food Intake**

**Importance of Accurate Tracking:** Accurate tracking helps identify whether you're sticking to your macronutrient targets and consuming the right portions.

**Tools and Techniques:**

**Use Apps:** Utilize food tracking apps to log and analyze your daily intake.

**Review Patterns:** Regularly review your food logs to identify any deviations from your planned intake.

**Incorporate Nutrient-Dense Foods**

**Focus on Quality:** Choose nutrient-dense foods that provide essential vitamins and minerals while keeping you in ketosis.

**Examples:**

**Leafy Greens:** Spinach, kale, and Swiss chard.

**Healthy Fats:** Avocados, olive oil, and nuts.

**Protein Sources:** Fatty fish, eggs, and grass-fed meats.

**Experiment with Carb Cycling**

**What is Carb Cycling?** Carb cycling involves alternating periods of low-carb intake with higher-carb days to boost metabolic flexibility.

**How to Implement:**

**Plan Higher-Carb Days:** Incorporate slightly higher-carb days once every week or two.

**Choose Healthy Carbs:** Opt for low-glycemic, keto-friendly carbs such as berries and sweet potatoes.

**Evaluate and Adjust Portion Sizes**

**Portion Control:** Ensuring that portion sizes are appropriate for your calorie and macronutrient goals can help overcome plateaus.

**Steps to Adjust:**

**Portion Size Review:** Assess your portion sizes and make adjustments if necessary.

**Use Tools:** Employ measuring tools or a food scale for more accurate portion control.

**Consider Meal Timing and Frequency**

**Meal Timing:** When you eat can affect metabolism and hunger levels.

Strategies:

**Intermittent Fasting:** Incorporate fasting periods to potentially enhance ketosis and appetite control.

**Regular Meals:** Keep your eating schedule regular to control your appetite and energy levels.

**Monitor and Address Stress and Sleep**

**Impact of Stress and Sleep:** Stress and poor sleep can impact metabolism and weight loss.

**Management Techniques:**

**Stress Reduction:** Engage in stress-relieving activities such as meditation or yoga.

**Sleep Hygiene:** Aim for 7-9 hours of quality sleep each night to support overall health and metabolism.

## Troubleshooting Digestive Issues and Cravings

Digestive issues and cravings can be significant challenges when following a Hyper Ketosis diet. Here's how to address and manage these concerns:

### Identifying and Managing Digestive Issues

**Common Digestive Issues:** Constipation, diarrhea, and bloating can occur when starting a ketogenic diet.

Solutions:

Increase Fiber Intake: Include keto-friendly fiber sources such as chia seeds, flaxseeds, and non-starchy vegetables.

Stay Hydrated: Water is a great way to aid with digestion and lessen bloating.

Electrolyte Balance: Ensure adequate intake of electrolytes (sodium, potassium, magnesium) to prevent digestive disturbances.

Digestive Enzymes: Consider taking digestive enzymes to help break down fats and proteins.

### Managing Cravings and Appetite

**Understanding Cravings:** Cravings for non-keto foods can be challenging and may arise due to hormonal changes or emotional triggers.

### Strategies to Manage:

**Healthy Alternatives:** Keep keto-friendly snacks available to address cravings without breaking ketosis.

**Mindful Eating:** Practice mindful eating techniques to stay aware of hunger and fullness cues.

**Stay Occupied:** Engage in activities or hobbies to distract yourself from cravings.

### Dealing with Emotional Eating

**Emotional Eating Triggers:** Stress, boredom, and emotional distress can lead to overeating or reaching for non-keto foods.

### Solutions:

**Identify Triggers:** Recognize emotional triggers and find alternative coping strategies.

Healthy Habits: Develop healthy eating habits and stress management techniques.

Seek Support: Consider talking to a therapist or joining a support group for additional assistance.

### Balancing Macronutrients to Control Hunger

**Role of Macronutrients:** Proper balance of fats, proteins, and carbohydrates can influence hunger and satiety.

### Adjustments:

**Increase Fats:** Ensure a sufficient intake of fats to enhance satiety and curb hunger.

**Monitor Protein:** Adjust protein intake if hunger persists, ensuring it's not too high or too low.

Navigating a Hyper Ketosis diet involves various questions and concerns. This chapter addresses common queries to help you effectively manage and personalize your diet. By understanding these aspects, you can better align your diet with your goals and ensure a safe and successful ketogenic journey.

## Common Concerns About the Hyper Ketosis Diet

### What is Hyper Ketosis and How is it Different from Standard Ketosis?

**Hyper Ketosis:** Hyper Ketosis is an advanced state of ketosis where ketone levels are significantly elevated, often achieved through stricter carbohydrate restriction and higher fat intake.

**Difference:** Compared to standard ketosis, Hyper Ketosis typically involves more stringent dietary control to achieve higher levels of ketones in the blood.

### Will I Experience Side Effects on a Hyper Ketosis Diet?

**Common Side Effects:** Possible side effects include keto flu, digestive issues, and fatigue as your body adapts to ketosis.

**Mitigation:** Address these side effects by ensuring proper hydration, electrolyte balance, and gradually transitioning into the diet.

### How Long Does It Take to Achieve Hyper Ketosis?

**Timeline:** It can take several days to weeks to enter Hyper Ketosis, depending on individual metabolism, adherence to the diet, and lifestyle factors.

**Factors Influencing Time:** Consistency in dietary choices and monitoring ketone levels can impact the speed of achieving Hyper Ketosis.

### Can I Follow a Hyper Ketosis Diet if I Have a Medical Condition?

Medical Conditions: Certain conditions, such as diabetes or kidney issues, may require special considerations.

Consultation: Always consult with a healthcare provider before starting the diet to ensure it's safe and appropriate for your condition.

### How Can I Ensure I'm Getting Enough Nutrients on a Hyper Ketosis Diet?

**Nutrient Density:** Focus on incorporating a variety of nutrient-dense, keto-friendly foods to meet your vitamin and mineral needs.

**Supplementation:** Consider supplements for nutrients that may be lacking, such as magnesium or omega-3 fatty acids.

## How to get back into ketosis

Identify the Cause of the Disruption

Potential Causes: Common reasons include consuming hidden carbs, inadequate fat intake, or inconsistent tracking.

**Solution:** Review your recent food intake and lifestyle choices to identify and correct the cause.

### Adjust Your Diet to Re-enter Ketosis

**Immediate Actions:** Return to strict carbohydrate restriction and increase fat intake to encourage your body to resume ketosis.

**Tracking:** Use ketone testing strips or a ketone meter to monitor your levels and confirm you've re-entered ketosis.

### Reassess Macronutrient Ratios

**Review Ratios:** Ensure your macronutrient ratios are in line with the requirements for Hyper Ketosis.

**Adjustments:** If necessary, modify your fat, protein, and carbohydrate ratios to achieve the desired ketone levels.

### Stay Hydrated and Maintain Electrolyte Balance

**Hydration:** Drink plenty of water to support metabolic processes and help reestablish ketosis.

**Electrolytes:** Replenish electrolytes through foods or supplements to prevent imbalances.

### Consult a Professional if Needed

**Guidance:** If you're struggling to regain ketosis or facing persistent issues, seek advice from a nutritionist or dietitian specializing in ketogenic diets.

### Is Hyper Ketosis Safe for Everyone?

### General Safety

Safety for Most: Hyper Ketosis is generally safe for healthy individuals when properly managed and monitored.

Pre-existing Conditions: Those with certain medical conditions (e.g., kidney disease, severe metabolic disorders) should proceed with caution.

### Considerations for Special Populations

**Pregnant or Nursing Women:** Consult with a healthcare provider before starting Hyper Ketosis.

Children and Adolescents: The diet may not be appropriate for younger populations without professional guidance.

### Monitoring Health Markers

**Regular Check-ups:** Regularly monitor health markers such as blood glucose, cholesterol levels, and kidney function to ensure safety.

**Adjustments:** Make dietary adjustments based on your health status and feedback from medical professionals.

### Potential Risks and Benefits

**Benefits:** Potential benefits include improved weight management, better blood sugar control, and increased energy levels.

Risks: Possible risks include nutrient deficiencies, electrolyte imbalances, and digestive issues if not managed properly.

### How to Personalize Your Plan

### Assess Your Individual Needs

**Health Goals:** Identify your specific health goals, whether they are weight loss, improved energy, or better metabolic health.

**Lifestyle Factors:** Consider your activity level, daily routine, and personal preferences.

## Customize Macronutrient Ratios

**Personalization:** Adjust fat, protein, and carbohydrate ratios based on your individual needs and how your body responds.

Be open to experimenting with different ratios to find what works best for you.

## Incorporate Personal Preferences and Tolerances

**Food Preferences:** Choose foods you enjoy and can sustain long-term.

**Food Tolerances:** Pay attention to how different foods affect your digestion and overall well-being.

## Set Realistic Goals and Monitor Progress

**Goal Setting:** Establish clear, achievable goals for weight loss, health improvement, or fitness.

**Tracking:** Regularly track your progress and make adjustments as needed based on your results and feedback.

## Seek Professional Advice

**Nutritionist or Dietitian:** Consult with a professional to tailor the diet to your specific health needs and goals. Ongoing Support: Engage with a healthcare provider or support group for ongoing guidance and motivation.

**How do I know if I'm in Hyper Ketosis?**

**Answer:** Use a ketone meter or ketone strips to measure your ketone levels in the blood, urine, or breath. Elevated ketone levels indicate Hyper Ketosis.

**Can I drink alcohol on a Hyper Ketosis diet?**

**Answer:** Alcohol can impact ketosis. Opt for low-carb options like dry wines or spirits, but consume in moderation.

**How often should I test my ketone levels?**

**Answer:** Testing frequency can vary. Some test daily, while others may test a few times a week, especially when adjusting the diet.

**What are the best snacks to eat while in Hyper Ketosis?**

**Answer:** Snacks should be low-carb and high in fat, like nuts, seeds, cheese, and avocado.

**How can I manage hunger on a Hyper Ketosis diet?**

**Answer:** Ensure adequate fat intake, stay hydrated, and consider incorporating fiber-rich keto-friendly foods to promote satiety.

**Can I eat fruit on a Hyper Ketosis diet?**

**Answer:** Most fruits are high in carbohydrates and should be limited or avoided. However, small amounts of berries may be included in moderation.

**What should I do if I experience muscle cramps on the diet?**

**Answer:** Muscle cramps may be due to electrolyte imbalances. Ensure adequate intake of potassium, magnesium, and sodium.

**How can I deal with bad breath while in ketosis?**

**Answer:** Bad breath is a common side effect of ketosis. Drinking water, chewing sugar-free gum, and maintaining good oral hygiene can help.

**Is it necessary to take supplements on a Hyper Ketosis diet?**

**Answer:** Supplements such as electrolytes, omega-3 fatty acids, and vitamin D may be beneficial, but consult a healthcare provider for personalized advice.

**Can I combine Hyper Ketosis with intermittent fasting?**

**Answer:** Yes, intermittent fasting can complement Hyper Ketosis by further promoting ketosis and enhancing fat burning.

**What are the best types of exercise while on a Hyper Ketosis diet?**

**Answer:** Low to moderate-intensity exercises like walking, swimming, and resistance training are generally well-suited for those in ketosis.

**How does Hyper Ketosis impact mental clarity and focus?**

**Answer:** Many individuals report improved mental clarity and focus due to stable energy levels provided by ketones.

**Can I follow a Hyper Ketosis diet if I have a thyroid condition?**

**Answer:** Consult with a healthcare provider, as thyroid conditions may require special dietary considerations or adjustments.

**When following a hyper-ketotic diet, how should I approach social settings and eating out?**

**Answer:** Plan ahead by reviewing restaurant menus, opting for low-carb dishes, and communicating your dietary needs to friends and family.

**Can I gain weight while following a Hyper Ketosis diet?**

**Answer:** While Hyper Ketosis can promote fat loss, excessive calorie intake from fats or other non-keto foods can lead to weight gain.

**How do I manage insulin levels on a Hyper Ketosis diet?**

**Answer:** The diet typically helps stabilize insulin levels, but monitor your levels regularly, especially if you have insulin sensitivity or diabetes.

**Can children follow a Hyper Ketosis diet?**

**Answer:** Children should only follow such a diet under strict medical supervision to ensure appropriate growth and development.

**What role does sleep play in achieving and maintaining Hyper Ketosis?**

**Answer:** Getting quality sleep helps your metabolism and can support staying in ketosis and overall health.

**Can I have caffeine on a Hyper Ketosis diet?**

**Answer:** Caffeine is generally acceptable in moderation, but be cautious of high-carb additives like sugar or flavored syrups.

**How does stress affect ketosis?**

**Answer:** Chronic stress can impact hormone levels and metabolism, potentially affecting ketosis. Implement stress management techniques for optimal results.

**Are there any common pitfalls to avoid on a Hyper Ketosis diet?**

**Answer:** Common pitfalls include hidden carbs in processed foods, inadequate fat intake, and inconsistent tracking of macronutrients.

**How do I handle cravings for non-keto foods?**

**Answer:** Address cravings by focusing on keto-friendly alternatives, staying hydrated, and understanding your hunger cues.

**What should I do if I experience diarrhea on a Hyper Ketosis diet?**

**Answer:** Diarrhea can occur due to increased fat intake. Ensure adequate fiber intake and consider adjusting fat sources or using digestive enzymes.

**Can I use artificial sweeteners on a Hyper Ketosis diet?**

**Answer:** Some artificial sweeteners are acceptable if they don't affect ketone levels. Opt for keto-friendly options like stevia or erythritol.

**How can I prevent nutrient deficiencies on a Hyper Ketosis diet?**

**Answer:** Include a variety of nutrient-dense foods, consider supplements, and regularly review your diet with a healthcare provider.

**How does Hyper Ketosis impact physical performance?**

**Answer:** Performance may initially decrease as your body adapts, but many individuals report improved endurance and energy over time.

**Can I use meal delivery services while on a Hyper Ketosis diet?**

**Answer:** Yes, but ensure the service offers keto-friendly options and review ingredient lists to maintain your dietary goals.

**How can I manage digestive issues related to increased fat intake?**

**Answer:** Gradually increase fat intake, use digestive aids if needed, and monitor your body's response to dietary changes.

**What are the long-term effects of following a Hyper Ketosis diet?**

**Answer:** Long-term effects vary by individual. Monitor your health markers regularly and consult with a healthcare provider for ongoing evaluation.

**Can I transition off a Hyper Ketosis diet gradually?**

**Answer:** Yes, gradually increasing carbohydrate intake while monitoring ketone levels can help ease the transition off the diet.

Made in United States
Orlando, FL
15 March 2025

59492483R00059